As a youth, John Nunes committed his life to improving others' existence. In his book *Meant for More*, he has succeeded in providing readers with an opportunity to enrich their lives by engaging the divine through the ordinary—through the homeless woman who unnerves, the nameless man at the bus stop, or our own colleagues and family members. Employing the words and thoughts of Luther and Augustine, among other theologians, Nunes provides a view of the world as it could be even though it is not. As the author states, the volume is not the definitive word, but a summons to "something more"; his book is such a charming invitation that any reader serious about the Christian journey dare not miss it.

Dr. Nancy Blattner, president, Fontbonne University

Those who know John Nunes already know the electricity of his way with words. Here, it is sparked by one four-letter word. *More*. Sending us on a breathtaking trek from Africa to Iowa, from our everyday routines to the most significant parts of our lives, this book does not leave us wanting more, but seeing more: more of God at work in the world and alive in the beating rhythms of our own hearts.

Rev. Dr. Travis Scholl, managing editor of seminary publications,
Concordia Seminary, St. Louis

John Nunes's candid and intimately perceptive grasp of the depth, beauty, and promise of the seemingly ordinary and mundane will lift us to live deeply and with purpose. Engaging and readable, *Meant for More* is best savored in short reads, permitting space for Nunes's mastery of vivid prose to inspire, challenge, and convict.

Ezer Kang, PhD, associate professor of psychology, Howard University

Dr. John Nunes's keen insights, hope, and Christ-centered message shine through in his writings. During these trying times of uncertainty, isolation, and swift transitions, it is wonderful to have this contribution for guidance and recalibration. As a Gen X pastor's wife and mother of five African American sons (three in college) during this physical and social pandemic, [I find] Dr. Nunes's book a welcome counsel. I eagerly anticipate learning how I, through the power of God, can be more in every aspect of my life.

Mrs. Shikina Bodley, woman of God, wife, and mother

To those dissatisfied souls plagued by social isolation in this digital age and those searching for purpose, this book is for you. Nunes shows that only Jesus can quench our thirst for satisfaction and give us meaning in life—found only in, with, and under His cross and blood-bought promises. Nunes brings a timely message and encouragement that exudes the sweetness of the Gospel accompanied by Lutheran theology and social ethics. Nunes shows God is calling us to be difference-makers, to speak up against injustice, to advocate for the minority, and to strive for "we" instead of "I."

Nokukhanya "Noks" Shabalala, MA, Concordia Seminary, St. Louis

In this graceful and uplifting book, John Nunes draws on his experience as a pastor, leader, and educator to deliver profound insights about how best to live completely and serve others. His deep faith and powerful observations combine to produce a work that will serve as a guidebook for those seeking inspiration, especially during these challenging times.

Dr. Freeman A. Hrabowski III, president, University of Baltimore, Maryland County

I love the voice of John Nunes. I have been blessed to hear it in coffee shops, conference rooms, and churches over the years. I am grateful that many others can now hear his voice in the pages of this new book. With immediate relevance for our cultural moment and the beauty of a well-written word, *Meant for More* explores what it might look like for Christians to choose a different, more ancient path of engagement with the world. John is a faithful guide down that path, marshaling the weight of Church history, the insights of the Lutheran tradition, and the heart-quickening Word of God to support his call to push into the unrest of our present age and bear witness to the age to come as it is already breaking in, with, and under the world we inhabit. I heartily commend this book.

Rev. Eric Landry, senior pastor, Redeemer Presbyterian Church,
Austin, TX, and editorial director, White Horse Inn

In *Meant for More*, Dr. Nunes helps us put a Gospel finger on what's missing in our lives. By pointing us to Christ and Christlike living, he shows us how we can find true meaning and escape the nagging, aching sense of emptiness that often consumes us. Thoughtful, funny, and accessible, *Meant for More* offers not only a diagnosis of the condition that we all experience but also the solution: finding our identity not in ourselves, but in Jesus Christ.

Rev. Hans Fiene, creator of Lutheran Satire

MEANT FOR MORE

In, With, and Under the Ordinary

JOHN ARTHUR NUNES

CONCORDIA PUBLISHING HOUSE · SAINT LOUIS

Published by Concordia Publishing House
3558 S. Jefferson Avenue, St. Louis, MO 63118-3968
1-800-325-3040 • cph.org

Library of Congress Cataloging-in-Publication Data

Names: Nunes, John, author.
Title: Meant for more : in, with and under the ordinary / John Arthur
    Nunes.
Description: Saint Louis, MO : Concordia Publishing House, 2020. | Summary:
    "Meant for More is uniquely sacramental-namely, that God's promise is
    effective "in, with, and under" ordinary means, including the Word of
    God. The tone will be written in a winsome and accessible way, yet it
    will be firmly grounded within the theology of the cross. Includes
    full-color graphics"-- Provided by publisher.
Identifiers: LCCN 2020022111 (print) | LCCN 2020022112 (ebook) | ISBN
    9780758665317 (paperback) | ISBN 9780758665324 (ebook)
Subjects: LCSH: Christian life.
Classification: LCC BV4501.3 .N86 2020 (print) | LCC BV4501.3 (ebook) |
    DDC 248.4--dc23
LC record available at https://lccn.loc.gov/2020022111
LC ebook record available at https://lccn.loc.gov/2020022112

1   2   3   4   5   6   7   8   9   10   29   28   27   26   25   24   23   22   21   20

CONTENTS

Dedication

HE TAUGHT ME HOW TO TIE MY SHOES,
SAY MY PRAYERS, DO GOOD,
FIGHT FOR TRUTH,
BE MESMERIZED BY BEAUTY,
LAUGH OUT LOUD,
NOT FOLLOW THE CROWD,
AND ABOVE ALL THINGS, TRUST GOD.
MY FIRST AND BEST HERO,

NEVILLE LEWISTON NUNES
(1931—2016)

THE SENSE THAT
THERE IS SOMETHING MORE
PRESSES IN. . . . OUR AGE IS
VERY FAR FROM SETTLING IN TO A
COMFORTABLE UNBELIEF. . . .
THE UNREST CONTINUES
TO SURFACE.

CHARLES TAYLOR,
A Secular Age

When I was an eighteen-year-old new immigrant to the US,[1] within me bubbled up an untried, untested confidence that I could change the world. I was under the spell of striving to commit my life to something constructive to improve lives. Yes, for others, but also for myself. No one could tell me I was *not* meant for more—but I hoped to position myself so that this "more" might positively overflow into the lives of others as well. There are few better beliefs to animate the dreams of young people than imagining themselves making a concrete and positive impact. And in the early 1980s, there seemed to me no better home base for an overeager optimist than "the States." Despite my clumsiness of overconfidence—founded on little more than naivete and faith—I was welcomed into the United States of America by those who took a risk on me, a double immigrant of mixed parentage. It's important to name names. It's critical to remember by name in prayers of thanksgiving those who blessed us in life. My depth of gratitude this side of heaven could never be depleted toward several professors at Concordia University, Ann Arbor. Those yet living—such as Mossman, Looker, Kalmes—and those who bask in eternity's sunrise—such as Heckert, Soovik, and Hackmann. Then there was a hearty band of believers from St. John Lutheran in inner-city Detroit: the Wagners, Bertha and George Steinke, Paul Schmidt, Mary Hillman, Mary Hunter, Wardell Polk, Henry Fann, Caroline Champine, James Robinson, and Helen Ellington.

My employment and academic focus for nearly four decades of adulthood has centered on faith-based, nonprofit, Lutheran-Christian

---

1   Prior to my becoming a US citizen, it happened more than once that, due to my lack of finances, failure to accurately understand immigration information, or lack of adequate advocacy, my status lapsed, and I would have been considered "undocumented," a potentially deportable, naturalized Canadian—especially since I was born in Jamaica.

organizations that provide options for life transformation through education, international humanitarianism, urban congregational life, and community development. I'm proud to currently be a resident of the Village of Bronxville in the New York City area, a place that feels like home to me, a region replete with what I consider the best (and some of the worst) that the world has to offer when it comes to diversity, culture, the arts, verve, media, dynamism, big business, and moreover, with missional opportunities galore—exceeding anywhere I've lived. My vocation here resonates with my soul as I breathe a sigh of vocational alignment at Concordia College—New York.

STRATEGIZING MORE

With God-ward Words

Every writer hoping to prepare words to be digested by others will have an avid appetite for worldly observation. A writer of faith, however, takes up differently "the pen of a skillful writer" (Psalm 45:1 NIV) when working with words. Hungrily observing this world, indeed, but a Christian writer's creative sphere is that thin slice of life between the world *as it is* and the world as it *ought to be*; the Christian writer's eyes knife along that narrative spectrum between secularity and spirituality. These writers tell stories of a world with a God at work *in, with, and under* the structures and substances of life; their sensitivities live between being both content with the beauty of this world and devastatingly restless about the ugliness that happens in it (Romans 12:2). Such writers proclaim the faith with deep conviction yet possess an honest palate for the places where faith has gone wrong and the faithful have done wrong. Their faith gives them an instinctive ear for the inflated language of exaggerated promises; in other words, they know the difference between mass-produced misinformation and the transcendent truth of the divine gift, which delivers what it promises, "a foretaste of the feast to come."[2] We have a God-ward Word, turning us with hopeful hearts toward our neighbors in love and turning us savingly toward God in faith.

---

2   *LSB*, Post-Communion Collect.

I have worked with words—sermonically, academically, devotionally, and inspirationally—since I was an undergraduate in college. I love the way words work, the way words work stylistically with other words, and the way working keenly with words serves to animate God's Word. But preparing words for reading and preparing words for hearing are two distinct art forms, one literary and the other rhetorical. Even though I have some forty years of experience at this, frequently I must remind myself that the eye and the ear receive words in vastly different ways. There is overlap, to be sure; however, few traps can ruin, say, a sermon faster than crafting it as if you were writing a theology textbook. Social media posts—at their best, which is rare—represent an emerging hybrid that attempts to merge speaking and writing. Blog posts especially convey this. The op-ed writer is evinced. Most of what you will read here, I have attempted to compose in a commonly accessible style that is written for this merger of the ear and the eye. At times, I play poetically with rhythm, rhyme, assonance, and alliteration. Certain sections might be best read aloud. I use colloquialisms as well as a few rarefied words that invite readers to stretch their vocabulary.

Martin Luther quipped rightly, "They say of writing that 'it only takes three fingers to do it'; but the whole body and soul work at it too."[3] This book is not intended to be an entire production, but an overture—an opening invitation to something more, perhaps a provocative entry to the more for which we are meant. This more will not come directly from the words contained in this book, but from the words that direct us toward another Word, the good Word, the *bene dictum*, a benediction that calls us into the world, into vocational action. This calling is impelled by the God-Word, you might say, who alone turns us God-ward in faith and praise and turns us world-ward in love and service. One day we will see God face-to-face; this will represent the ultimate culmination of that more for which we are meant. In, with, and under the inscripturated Word (the Bible), we see the incarnate Word (Jesus), the very face of God revealed, in whom we are discovered by grace and ourselves discover our meaningfulness.

This volume's vignettes and assertions do not intend to prescribe a superior nor a single biblical pattern for relating to the world. There is a

---

3   *LW* 46:249.

I MUST REMIND

MYSELF THAT THE EYE AND

THE EAR RECEIVE

WORDS IN DIFFERENT WAYS.

time for everything under the sun, and some may not find themselves in a vocation and location that permits the pattern of engagement I propose. But I write so that possibly the Holy Spirit may stir, spark, provoke, prompt a restlessness that leads to action, that leads to the Lord Jesus, that leads to life everlasting.

In, With, and Under

Once, when traveling for work with Lutheran World Relief (LWR), I heard this plea in a community we'd call (ironically) "backwater"— a metaphorical term referring to areas that have been economically bypassed, where the current of progress has not reached. While working in such a region plagued by drought and famine, we heard their request: "Just help us get water!"

Think of that threshold—"just water." When one of our daughters was a teenager, she had her cell phone privileges suspended for just cause: downloads—very dangerous and, at that time, quite expensive. Her response, at full volume, and I quote: "Arghhh! How I'm gonna live?"

In the remote high hills of Kenya, LWR oversaw the implementation of a water system. We could have just plopped in a well and said, "We did our part and met your water needs. Goodbye!" But Lutherans value working contextually within communities. It's a practical application of the in, with, and under principle: pitching tents in the soil of others, like the God-man of John 1:14, walking together and talking together, sharing our deepest woes, fighting together our spiritual foes—the enemies of human flourishing—accompanying them with reciprocal respect as they accompany us, through the terrifying absurdities, through the dust and sand and soil and ashes in the deepest valleys of despair, building community with them, employing a critical and self-critical process of discovery. This way of working helped LWR arrive together at the mutual conclusion: "just give us water . . . we'll do the work, and God will give the growth."

Annastasia was the country program manager in Kenya when water arrived. In New Testament Greek, her name literally means "resurrection" or "to stand again." Annastasia lived out the meaning of her name in actions, working for justice, human dignity, and peace, and yes, representing US Lutherans, but even more representing that Resurrected One, the One who as God but also as a human being sits, even as you read these words, at the right hand of the divine power (to use the biblical metaphor), the One who is the source and the summit yet holds together all things, His Church and our congregations and our families and our communities and all our organizations that want to do more for the world. Jesus Christ holds together our entire fragile world. Arthur Carl Piepkorn once wrote that this Jesus Christ is the pivotal One whose life, death, resurrection, and promised return makes "ultimate sense of . . . [our] terrifying absurdities"[4]—including not having access to basic, life-giving necessities, such as water.

Annastasia understands her ministry as bringing commonsense solutions. With indomitable faith, she works day after day so that the poorest of the poor, too, can "stand again." She told me when I visited Nairobi that "development is the story behind the well." What first appears to be the solution often conceals a deeper story.

In, with, and under it all, God comes to us through ordinary means, ordinary water, ordinary wine, and the ordinary hands of ordinary women and men like you and me and Annastasia in order to do more than we could ask or imagine (Ephesians 3:20). Jesus' saving words point to Himself for human good: "If anyone thirsts, let him come to Me and drink. Whoever believes in Me, as the Scripture has said, 'Out of his heart will flow rivers of living water'" (John 7:37–38).

A Counterpoint Rather Than a Counterpunch

Because of sin, the relationship between Christians and this world is plagued by a tension that can lead to false absolutes. At the extremes, we can either withdraw from culture or become overinvested in . . . let's call it the symphony of life. I will be using an extended musical metaphor here. Sometimes, Christians position themselves exclusively as a countercultural movement, a group of believers who instinctively

---

4   Arthur Carl Piepkorn, "The One Eucharist for the One World," *Concordia Theological Monthly* 43, no. 2 (February 1972): 101, https://media.ctsfw.edu/Text/ViewDetails/9236.

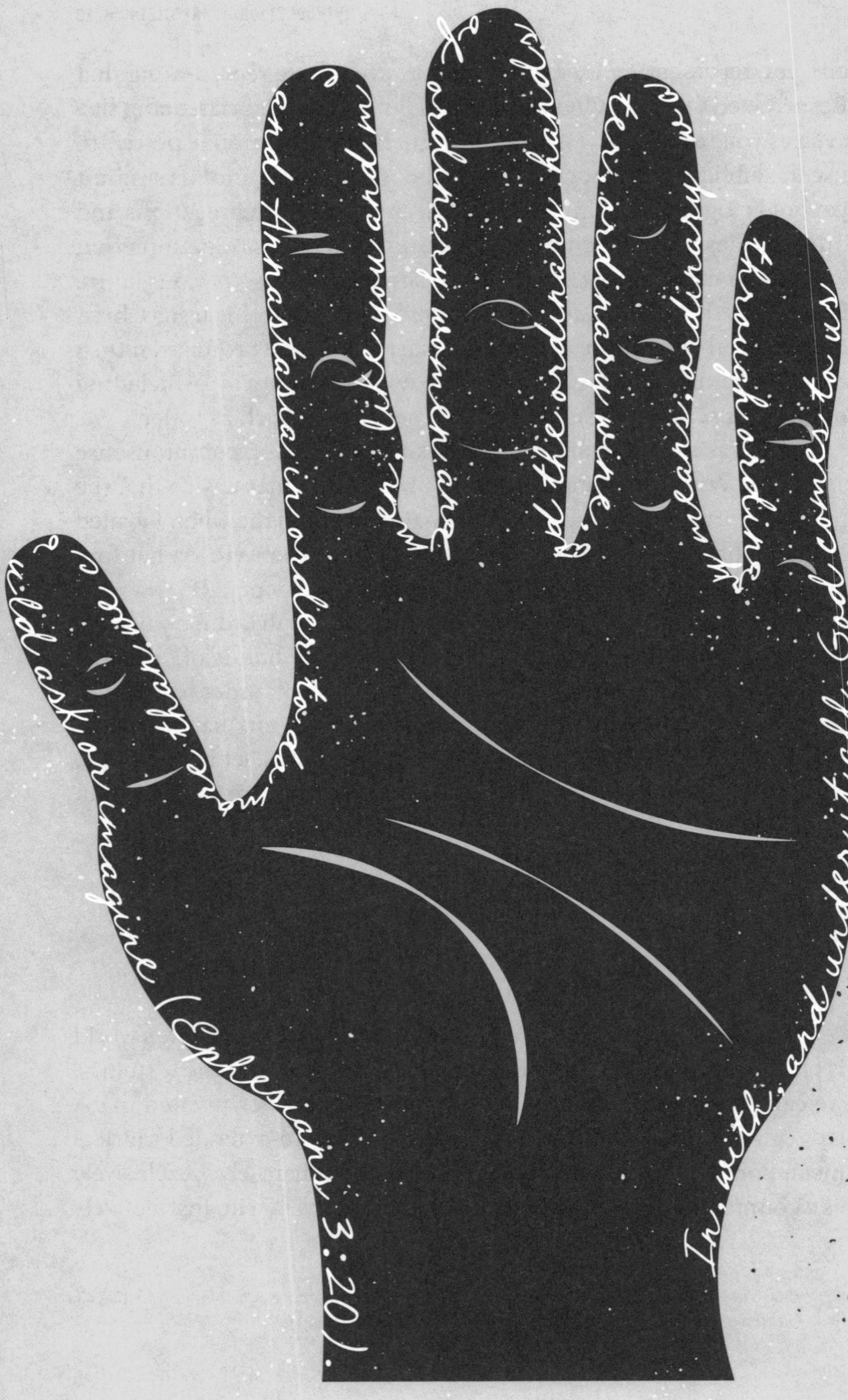
In, with, and under it all, God comes to us
through ordinary
means, ordinary wa
ter, ordinary wine,
d the ordinary hands
ordinary women and
men, like you and m
e and Anastasia in order to do
more than we co
uld ask or imagine (Ephesians 3:20).

go against the grain of this world whatever the issue, taking on a defensive posture, poised always to counterpunch with those who don't share our beliefs in a perceived cultural boxing match (*Kulturkampf*). Yet, an ancient and contrasting perspective might be for Christians to see ourselves (as well as to hear others) as more in counterbalance. There is a mutual neediness between salt and flavorlessness, between light and darkness, between leaven and a lump of dough. The absence of one helps us to realize the presence of the other; they symbolize a mystical, mutual interdependence.

Think of the idea of *contrapunctus*, or counterpoint, in Western music. This technique suggests musical parts that are harmonically interdependent yet independent in terms of melody and movement. Think of harmony as the vertical dimension of music and melody as the horizontal dimension. We need both. What I propose represents an Augustinian both/and approach, an approach that focuses on being both *in* the world but not *of* the world, a paradoxical engagement. This counterpoint perspective does not eliminate difference, disagreement, and dissonance. Rather, it acknowledges them and aims to engage in conversation, dialogue, even debate for the sake of the redemption—not the destruction—of the other.

Some, however, are wired more aggressively, like the ancient Manicheans. They might suggest that this view represents a compromise or commingling of the truth. Certainly, the same accusations were made of Jesus, of His cavorting with the enemy, of His guilt by associating with "undesirables." Admittedly, Jesus' ability to successfully differentiate Himself from sinful influences exceeds ours; we too often fall short. While our connection to the transcendent can't compare to Jesus', like Him, we can make an impact only when we are connected with the world. How can we bring beauty to this world's music if we are disconnected? At the level of our soul, our connectedness finds courage to do more than fit in, to be more than singers of the same old song, but to be the virtuosos we were meant to be, creative voices displaying the most orthodox version of our faith, bringing to the world our unique musicality with instrumental conviction, joining the symphony of life wholeheartedly to the glory of God. "Whatever your hand finds to do, do it with your might" (Ecclesiastes 9:10)!

Called, Gathered, Enlightened, Sent, and Confident

HOLY SPIRIT,
YOU HAVE **CALLED** US TO BE YOUR POETS OF THE POSSIBLE
IN SPITE OF THE TIMES WHEN LIFE FEELS ABSURDLY IMPOSSIBLE.

> **GATHERED** BY YOU, WE IMAGINE A FUTURE OF PEACE
> IN YOUR PERFECT EMPIRE;

> > UNTIL THEN, WE ARE **ENLIGHTENED** BY YOU
> > TO RESIST THE DIVISIVE TRIBAL TRUTHS OF OUR IMPERFECT WORLD,
> > INFECTED AS IT IS BY SIN, DEATH, AND THE DEVIL;

> > **SENT** BY YOU AS CARETAKERS OF THIS BROKEN WORLD,
> > WE REASSEMBLE THE FRAGMENTS OF YOUR FRACTURED CREATION.

BLESS US AS WE WORK IN, WITH, AND UNDER
THE WORLD JUST AS IT IS,
CONFIDENT THAT YOU ARE ALWAYS AT WORK
IN THE MIDDLE OF ALL THAT IS ORDINARY;
CONFIDENT THAT THROUGH OUR STRUGGLING,
YOU ARE TEACHING US ALL THINGS;
CONFIDENT THAT WE ALL ARE MEANT FOR MORE.

> IN THE NAME OF THE ONE FROM WHOM YOU COME,
> JESUS CHRIST, OUR LORD,
> WE COURAGEOUSLY GO FORTH IN FAITH.
> AMEN.

1

RECOMBOBULATING MORE

We live in a discombobulating world. What do we do in the face of unexpected disasters, unpredictable societal chaos, incontrovertible political divisiveness, inexplicable tragedies, unforeseen heartbreaks, unforeseeable breakups, hope-canceling disappointments, and grief that escapes words? The tough stuff dents our smooth plans, scrapes our confidence, and breaks our dreams. "Hope deferred makes the heart sick," the sage tells us in Proverbs 13:12.

It can feel like the life is sucked out of us, yet deep within us, we are haunted by the sense that these things are not a part of the plan for us, that we are meant for more. In some deep-down place of the soul, we are right.

At Milwaukee's Mitchell International Airport, there is a place you go *after* you endure the screening process. After disheveling oneself by removing pieces of clothing and forgotten metallic items, perhaps taking two or three trips through the TSA line, one can feel discombobulated. Fortunately, in this airport, there is an area on the other side that they call the Recombobulation Area.

That is my experience of the church—it's a place to get oneself recombobulated. God's grace, working through the Word, the Sacraments, and the community of faith, calls us and places us irrevocably within the orbit of the universal community of faith. The church constitutes the only place on earth I know committed to gathering the hopes and the dreams of those carrying life's heartsick deferrals (Proverbs 13:12) and uniting those deepest prayers with the timeless praise of all saints and every rank of angel. Think of the time-transcending enormity of that promise, especially when the earthly and heavenly choruses join one another in the Holy Eucharist. And because of what the church promises in Jesus Christ, put your glasses on, because God's got a future for you. "Surely there is a future, and your hope will not be cut off" (Proverbs 23:18). That's a recombobulating thought! Your future address will be the city that "has no need of sun or moon to shine on it, for the glory of God gives it light, and its lamp is the Lamb" (Revelation 21:23). You are meant for more.

Enduring More

I want to believe in God. Sometimes this leads to desperation. Oftentimes, this is humanly challenging, especially when bad things seem triumphant. Why does disaster strike? Why are there shootings of children at Sandy Hook Elementary in Newton, Connecticut, and in Parkland, Florida, and of people at prayer in Charleston, South Carolina, or Sutherland Springs, Texas, or Christchurch, New Zealand? When these things happen, some people try to connect the dots, like Job's friends in the Old Testament,[5] trying to make sense, to make meaning: "It must be something you've done, something in your past." I prefer an approach that has two steps: First, we recognize that life isn't always good, beautiful, or fair—not since the fatal fall from Eden's initial paradise. Second, we recognize that coming face-to-face with the consequences of life's crookedness provides us with teachable moments, chances to grow in grace. On the other hand, attempting to force sense out of tragedies can be as difficult as it is dangerous. Pronouncements that connect the dots of cause and effect don't help. Judging can lead to blind alleys of blaming victims or of falsely blaming victimizers or of misreading the context. There's always more than meets the eye.

---

5   Job's problematic friends Eliphaz, Bildad, and Zophar insist that Job's suffering is the result of divine punishment. They reason correctly that God is just, but conclude erroneously that Job's suffering, therefore, must be the result of an unjust action he has done and for which he must repent. Those who are suffering would do better to avoid these sorts of friends, regardless of their intention.

Of course, more academic types among us might see suffering as an occasion for conjecturing about large questions of theodicy, like the reasons for good and evil or the characteristics of God's all-goodness versus God's all-powerfulness. Rather, I strive to see suffering as a chance for Christians to respond, to hear cries of suffering as calls to action. We can endure more when we are actively engaged as part of the solution, as partners in action, as participants in the more for which we are meant.

A friend, Dean Wenthe, recently put it in a way that captured my imagination (and honestly made me shout in spontaneous joy): "God's grace outruns what we can behold." Think of yourself in a panic, running from a problem, out of breath, searching the horizon for help. God's grace has already been where you are, and it will never let you down. Once we accept that God's grace outruns the limits of human vision and knowledge, we can conclude the following: First, the problems that dominate our minds have already been worked out for our good by the unseen grace of a timeless God (Romans 8:28). Second, while we're fretting unnecessarily about the problems we see daily—unconcerned with those problems not yet in our view—the same grace of God has already run on ahead of us for the sake of our salvation to seize future problems and to use them to mold our character, way in advance of our awareness.

Flourishing More

That we are meant for more means more than just filling your life with more matter—more material goods, more stuff. It means filling our lives with more of what matters. Invest in what matters, in what promises permanence and transcendence, not transience and temporariness. "And the world is passing away along with its desires, but whoever does the will of God abides forever" (1 John 2:17).

That's the Christian counterbalance for these dispiriting times. The key to full human flourishing is not to fill your life with more pleasure, leisure, and treasures. Getting more, gaining more, acquiring more, earning more, hoarding more, feeling more pleasurable sensations does not result, in itself, in the more for which we are meant.

Meaning and significance are discovered by focusing on those things that are eternal and using our gifts to invest in redeeming pursuits in the present age. The more for which we're meant must be more than the mere pursuit of our desires. Throughout history, wise observers have described these earthly acquisitional and transactional pursuits as ephemeral, unsatisfying, and ultimately unattainable. Rather, we are discovered by our more as we pay more attention to the prepositions *in*, *with*, and *under*. By this I mean not that we find our more, but that the more intended for us finds us as we give ourselves away following an in, with, and under model: *in*—investing in others, being genuinely interested in their lives; *with*—standing with others for a cause, accompanying them, walking alongside them on their roads to Emmaus (Luke 24); and *under*—undergirding those who invite or need our support, advocating for them, struggling to understand their situation. These prepositions are used theologically to describe, in a way that exceeds rationality, the relationship between the presence of Jesus and the ordinary water, bread, and wine of the Sacraments.

This approach to life is decidedly sacramental, meaning that God's promise is discoverable in, with, and under ordinary means, including the ordinary language through which the Spirit spoke the inspired Word of God. This presence extends also to God's hidden work in the world (Isaiah 45:15), in which we are God's co-workers, often hidden, humble, and unnoticed, but always meant for more. This idea of presence suggests that in, with, and under the ordinary, the extraordinary weaves through with transcendent wonder. The divine is, indeed, in the details. Holiness is threaded through our seemingly mundane duties and everyday responsibilities. Every so-called run-of-the-mill vocation is a location of eternal significance, a sign of grace.

Not for Lutherans Only | PART 1

The life of the reformer Martin Luther illustrates a rhythm of varied engagement with a world of problems. There's a time for *dialogue*—as Luther sparked in Wittenberg, posting his point of view in order to start a public conversation about how individuals are saved by God. In this time to talk, there's discussion, asking questions and inviting

inquiries, sharing information and attempting to persuade others of your perspective.

There is also a time for *defiance*, as Luther demonstrated at Worms when he drew his line in the sand and said, "Here I stand!" The focus here is on right and wrong, on resisting what you've concluded is untruth, on balking, stubbornly refusing to continue.

Finally, there comes a time for *disengaging*—as Luther attempted at the Wartburg when he assumed a pseudonym and withdrew from society for the sake of survival and study. There is a time to walk away. Depending on your location and vocation in life, you might sense that now is the time for you to exercise the option of retreating from this world. While I respect that, I will propose the opposite. Now is the time to participate in, with, and under the institutions and individuals of this world on their path toward renewal. The way forward requires faithful wisdom and Christ-compelled courage, confident that you are aligned with the God "who desires all people to be saved and to come to the knowledge of the truth" (1 Timothy 2:4). The Holy Spirit works through our meaningful human engagement to bring about the divine design that God desires for all people.

Limping More

Almost two decades ago, six months after my fortieth birthday, I learned the difference between a rapture and a rupture. A *rapture* refers, as in 1 Thessalonians 4:17, to the return of Christ, and when you tear your Achilles tendon, the pain will make you wish that Jesus would return immediately. I was at Lutheran camp playing basketball when I nicked my ankle on the rim . . . of course I didn't; I barely got off the ground when the injury happened that taught me some important life lessons.

1. I learned how important it is to know your limits and live within them. Living within your limits is an opportunity to learn about a God without any limits. While we sense the fullness of the potential God has placed in our lives, we also are painfully aware that this potential seems impossible to

reach. In fact, the more profoundly we sense this, the more frustrated we can become. The spirit within is often prone to push the flesh beyond what is possible. Because of our innate pride, the fact that we are meant for more can sometimes trick us into attempting more than that for which we are meant. Injury can be the result.

2. I learned how to lean on others. Being in a wheelchair is an opportunity to learn how needy one is, how dependent one is on, say, one's family.

3. I learned, unfortunately, just how much God's people can be a lot like Job's friends. Especially when hard times come, there are some who think they can connect the dots about what went wrong in your life and what you did to deserve it.

4. But what I learned more than anything was that even when you're doing the work of the Lord, you can experience hard times. Six months later, just as I was healing, I was on stage speaking at a Lutheran youth gathering when I stepped into a six-inch gap between the risers on the stage. I subsequently retore that same Achilles tendon in front of six hundred youth who thought it was so cool that I wiped out on stage and was faking pain. This was no act; this was agony. And how did it happen? I mean, I was at an official event of The Lutheran Church—Missouri Synod. I was literally holding and teaching from a Bible. Doing the work of ministry is no immunity from hard times. Two leg-aching tears in six months while doing ministry!

Yes, hard times have come and will come to every town, every life, every location, but Jesus is already there. Jesus, who went to a wilderness of testing (Matthew 4:1–11)—driven by the Holy Spirit, mind you, into a barren time of temptation—is the same Jesus whom we believe is really, truly present here and now, Sunday in and Sunday out, in your place of worship and in every place where the people gather, where the Sacraments are celebrated, where the Word goes forth. Christ is there. When water is splashed in the name of Father, Son, and Spirit, Christ is there. When bread and wine are shared in connection with that Word, Christ is there. I believe our success in ministry in the future will require a radical faith in the real presence of Jesus, alongside us, in, with, and under our suffering. The more we realize the presence of Jesus, the more we will become as the people of Jesus. And even when, for whatever circumstances, we are prevented from gathering together, even when we may be suffering in our souls from a lack of Eucharistic fellowship, may that ache open us up to new ways to welcome outsiders into the way, the truth, and the life.

Jesus is present in His Body, the Church, this whole ragtag, occasionally bungling bundle of baptized humanity, who support one another and stand with one another, who strengthen one another to live out our community in Christ and not merely to affirm it, not merely to *talk* about it, but to *be* about it, and to be what we already are: a community of unity in Christ, united by God's vision of the church, not our own. In summary and characteristically, Luther puts it plainly: "Now, wherever you hear or see this word preached, believed, professed, and lived, do not doubt that the true *ecclesia sancta catholica*, 'a Christian holy people' must be there."[6] We can be more in Jesus and in the church.

Dancing More

Being downcast is not rare, but staying there is. We all have overcast phases of life; despite the shadows, you can still move forward in the light. I challenge you to consider recording your experience. Journal. Compose music or poetry. Create something. Even in your speechlessness, the Holy Spirit can locate language for you to share, if not now, later. Don't let your pain be in vain (Romans 8:26–27).

Sing your song. Live your dream. Believe your faith. Confess your conviction.

As necessary as it is to have lung function, a pulse, and brain waves, these obviously do not deliver the meaning and significance that make life worthwhile. I propose that the more for which we are meant is accessible only to those who are spiritually alive. Open your eyes. See

---

6   *LW* 41:150.

the difference between life with Christ in God and merely existing. Taste the difference between being biologically not dead and being a living being, living the life of the One who said, "I came that they may have life and have it abundantly" (John 10:10). We are meant by God to be more than a random combustion of genes and chromosomes, more than a mistake of history or an accident of biology; therefore, life is not lost first by heart or lung failure or the demise of neurologic activity, but long before that.

It ends when we are overtaken by a certain regret, that our love for self and for others was far too cramped, narrow, and hurried. What greater love seeks you today, promising to show you "a still more excellent way" (1 Corinthians 12:31), bidding you to leap into a life packed with passionate acts of service, purposeful relationships of love, and meaningful investments of sacrificial joy. Henry David Thoreau, the nineteenth-century abolitionist, tax resister, and poet, once sadly put it like this: "The mass of men lead lives of quiet desperation."[7]

Only you can refuse to be silenced by quiet desperation. Do a radical act and sing your song, dance your dance, dare your dream, live your life, be the more that God meant you to be. Your yesterday, your today, your tomorrow, your most ordinary of days, has already been recombobulated by the extraordinary power and strength of the One who delivers us from evil.

---

7   Thoreau, *Walden* (Boston: Ticknor and Fields, 1854), 10.

2

BELONGING MORE

ur beautiful but bent and demented world continues to need folks with the naive faith of difference-makers, with passionate integrity and compassionate intensity, like those we see in the March for Our Lives or Lutherans For Life; or like those I see daily—my "true-believer" colleagues invested in first-generation students, international students, and students from a multiplicity of backgrounds; or like those whom Paul describes as confident that God, "according to His power at work within us," is able to do much, much more "than all we ask or imagine" (Ephesians 3:20 NIV).

While we might, each of us, see ourselves as cosmopolites, global citizens, all of us are in fact called by the Holy Spirit to work in a particular place among a particular people. One's particular vocation usually points to a particular location. Particularity produces authenticity.

A literary friend—whose identity is best kept anonymous—reported his situation with these words: "My world consists of concentric circles of performance, masquerades. While some degree of theatrical fakeness is necessary to survive—authenticity can become a bloody mess—when there is no escape valve, people explode in stupidity. In the circle that's closest to you, you need something that's real and respectful, intimate and forgiving, sometimes even stupidly playful. Without it, you die of artificiality and artifice. You are a human, after all, very human."

This is the church at its best, a place of authenticity and hospitality—a place that's unsurprised by the realities of life, unembarrassed by human foibles, a place where we can call a thing what it is, where you can bring your personal terrors, your workplace troubles, and your tantrum-throwing toddlers. Welcoming others searching for their more is not optional at church.

There is evidence that young people are returning to church, but not necessarily the church of their parents' choice; nor are they drawn to doctrine or attracted primarily to the promises of eternal salvation—though indisputably doctrinal theology is central to the confession of Jesus Christ. "They are drawn to churches where they find a sense of belonging and that show care for their 'neighbor,' the people of the world, and God's creation. Young adults active in congregations also look for solid, coherent doctrine that is consistently applied for the good of others."[8] They're affiliating and not necessarily "joining" in the membership sense. They're connecting because churches provide community as a bulwark against loneliness. They are looking for more in life, and they find it in a group with a social or communal cause as mitigation against meaninglessness.

Martin Luther puts his finger on a primary witness to attract those who struggle to belong. It does not consist of extraordinarily refined dialogue about doctrinal matters—though that's why people eventually remain rooted in the fellowship. Our teachings are not initially what first attracts them. It's about an ordinary lifestyle witness, when acts of faith permeate through and percolate up in, with, and under daily life:

> **When we bear no one a grudge, entertain no anger, hatred, envy, or vengefulness toward our neighbors, but gladly forgive them, lend to them, help them, and counsel them; when we are not lewd, not drunkards, not proud, arrogant, overbearing, but chaste, self-controlled, sober, friendly, kind, gentle, and humble; when we do not steal, rob, are not usurious, greedy, do not over-charge, but are mild, kind, content, charitable; when we are not**

---

8   Mark Kiessling (director of Youth Ministry for The Lutheran Church—Missouri Synod), email message to author, May 16, 2020. See also *Relationships Count: Engaging and Retaining Millennials* (CPH and The Lutheran Church—Missouri Synod, 2019).

false, mendacious, perjurers, but truthful, trustworthy, and do whatever else is taught in these commandments.[9]

And these good works that Luther describes have a built-in boomerang effect. The deeds done in love that we send out to draw others in also eventually return to us as blessings: "Whoever desires to love life and see good days, let him keep his tongue from evil and his lips from speaking deceit" (1 Peter 3:10).

Not Alone

It's not easy to remain buoyant and joyful when you consider the malaise among many mainline churches, the downward trajectory in demographics in which we seem to find ourselves, the thinning of memberships, their fiscal challenges, the graying of members, and our rather monochromatic ethnic makeup. We know we are meant for more. We know we are called to be an all-nations mission. We confess our faith in the *one* church, yet as denominations, we too often see ourselves irreconcilably divided.

Late one evening, there was a storm in the life of one of our five daughters. A relationship had ended badly. Her sense of rejection was raw. Rumors were being circulated by her ex that attacked her character. This text message was urgent. In response to this message, I replied with a note I hoped would bring comfort and perspective to a daughter who felt unmoored, unconnected, "unfaired" against, alone:

> No matter how much good you try to do, in this world some people will not like you. Perhaps they feel indicted by your commitments, but the inevitability of attracting haters seems strangely to increase the more you stand for a cause that's true. Over time, however, if you stay your course, no matter how much you're discredited, the people you truly need, the right people, will invest in you, respect you, and love you for what you strive to be and to do. And the high quality of this support, earned

---

9 *LW* 41:166.

the hard way, not only will get you through your tough times but will take you to a place of beauty amidst life's ugliness. So, sing your song, follow the Conductor, do good, walk in truth. A beautiful rhythm accompanies you, and beautiful people will be attracted to the beauty of the Lord they see in you! You belong!

My experience tells me that "the right people," those who will invest in her, are the people of faith, the church. My faith tells me that it's all beyond me who belongs, who's in and who's out. Because salvation is entirely God's work in Jesus Christ, not mine, but beyond my own understanding or ability. It's beyond me that I myself belong to Christ and that I belong to others (whom I may not even like) who also belong to Christ. As Martin Luther stresses, "The Holy Spirit does not take possession of me in isolation from other Christians."[10] This thought of belonging more both comforts my loneliness and confronts my coldness toward others. Assured that I belong to Jesus Christ, how am I creating avenues for others to belong as well? Luther put it more emphatically: "For outside of the Christian Church there is no truth, no Christ, no salvation."[11] Belonging might be a matter of eternal life and eternal death, so let's do everything to help outsiders find their way in.

These students of Jesus in the Gospels, these followers of Jesus called disciples, were enrolled in a three-year course with front-row seats to the life of Jesus. Imagine being an eyewitness and an ear-witness to the Son of God performing signs and wonders. They saw it with their own eyes, and yet the Gospel writer tells us that they, even they, still needed their minds opened to understand the Scriptures (Luke 24:45–48). They couldn't get it without mind-opening intervention. How can we expect to get it without some help from above? That's why I go to church.

---

10 Charles Arand, *That I May Be His Own* (St. Louis: Concordia Publishing House, 2000), 163.

11 *LW* 75:254.

Connecting More

We reside in a culture with more amusements than ever, yet we report more of what feels like boredom more often, or at least what feels like more than ever before. We navigate a life path of more hyperconnectedness than ever, yet we're more alone and anonymous to others, feeling unknown and uncared for; more interconnected than ever, yet more disconnected from meaning, purpose, and self-worth. Residing in a global village, we are tied together by technology and transportation, yet happiness and wholeness seem more elusive than ever; we are hyperlinked to others technologically, yet disconnected from one another, from our ancestors, from our families, from our children, even from our own selves. Some of us surf social media looking for a cause to believe in, a face to relate to, a relationship to trust. What Christians call "sin" creeps into all of our lives. We all miss the mark. We all fall short of the more for which we are meant. Even the most noble of birds in flight, especially if afflicted or fatigued, is not above landing on an ignoble tree.

On Thursday, May 25, 1995, I was driving in Detroit, listening to National Public Radio. So stunned was I by two back-to-back news stories that I pulled over and jotted down the sequence. The first report was that of the first full-length movie shown entirely on the internet, called *Cyberstalker*. The second was the announcement of the imminent end of the *Baltimore Evening Sun* that upcoming September. Though this was a quarter of a century ago, the implications were obvious. New electronic media were beginning to ease out older media such as newspapers.

When this storied newspaper ended its publication, it reported that the reasons had to do with the ways in which the news appetites of the public were changing. The demand was rising for instant and continuous reporting because of a change in the pace of life. Newspapers were not being read by their traditional constituencies because of the changes in the lives of blue-collar workers and the role of women in the workplace. The tempo of life had accelerated. The irony is that the computer in our pockets giving us instantaneous access to a world of information and immediate connectivity has not slowed the rat-race pace. People feel more rushed than ever.

Our Western culture is highly digitized, technologically confident, overconnected. Seemingly savvy, we are overloaded with an abundance of information, data in the form of bits and bytes; however, there is something missing. We are increasingly more isolated, lonely, alienated, frustrated, depressed, and suicidal than perhaps any other culture in the planet's history.

The opportunities for evangelistic witness, compassionate outreach, and genuine catholic connectivity are connected to the human need for community in the face of a disconnectivity that defiles and defaces the dignity of humans. First, we see that you are meant and then seek the more for those to whom we're sent.

Welcoming More

"I am fatigued by life!" "Have you seen the chaos I live in?" We share our competing complexities. In the midst of all in which we find ourselves, who has time to do much more than fake like you care about another's struggles? Feigning authenticity can approach comedic levels. You can be so real you become fake. You can be so welcoming you come across with an insincerity that chases others away.

What specific practices of hospitality both sustain us and help us welcome others in Jesus' name? In light of the decline of "traditional institutions," Facebook vows to build supportive, safe, informed, civically engaged, and inclusive communities.

The text about guests who came to Sodom (Genesis 19) is most ostensibly used to support prohibitions against same-sex relationships. That same narrative is vastly underrecognized for what it reveals about the morality of hospitality. Luther's commentary on this story does not miss this point, that an underlying sin of Sodom was "utmost smugness"—the fact that "they live in luxury and do violence to their guests" rather than welcoming and sheltering threatened strangers.[12] He sees Lot, the host, taking initiative to provide a safe space in his

---

12 *LW* 3:238.

own home for travelers under siege: "He is looking for guests and is aware of the raging of the citizens and of their deeds of violence. Therefore if some strangers should come, he wants them to stay with him, where they can spend the night free from abuse and violence."[13]

In an ecclesial environment of competing moralities, rife with bantering over whose virtuosity is more virtuous, churches that aim to be both evangelical and catholic, scriptural and confessional, focus wisely on the virtue of hospitality as they listen to others, welcoming them in Jesus' name, even with the diversities we may find dizzying. It is not our job to change people so that God can accept them; it is our job to accept people so that God, by grace, through faith, working through the Spirit, can change them. As Luther reassures us, the church belongs to Jesus Christ: "We are not the ones who can preserve the church, nor were our forefathers able to do so. Nor will our successors have this power. . . . We are not the church's guardians. . . . If it were up to us, the church would perish before our very eyes, and we together with it."[14]

Knowing that the church's success does not depend upon us is liberating. It frees us from the trap, from the very Western penchant for overconfidence, so that we can authentically embrace others in response to the embrace of grace we ourselves have received. Yes, we are meant to be more welcoming, but no strategy or tactic of welcoming can save us or the church, especially if that pathway is determined by individual initiative.

Collaborating More

Institutions get a bad rap. Institutionalization, even worse! But if we think about institutions as systems for us to work together, structures for us to co-labor, opportunities for us to collaborate more, perhaps we can understand better their positive function. The upside of institutions is that they provide continuity and endurance for our individual

---

13   *LW* 3:244; I'd like to credit Dr. Leopoldo A. Sánchez from Concordia Seminary, St. Louis, for alerting me to Luther's insight.

14   *LW* 47:118.

projects and personal passions. When we join with others, when we collaborate more, we become more.

The ministry of Jesus Christ Himself has endured for millennia not only because of the ongoing presence and power of the Holy Spirit, but also because His saving work became codified, systematized, credalized, enacted by, and embedded within the liturgies, sermons, songs, and Sacraments of the one holy catholic and apostolic church.

We all fall for the temptation to whine about the downside of the grinding institutionalization of the church—argh! the red tape, silly administrivia, life-sucking policies, slow decision-making processes, the meetings. As one of my early supervisors frequently complained, "Any simple problem can be made unsolvable if you have enough meetings to discuss it."

All of this, in part, constitutes the price we pay for collaboration. Or think of it this way: institutions are investments in longevity and endurance; to work well, they require from each of us the humble admission "I don't know everything, nor can I be everywhere at the same time, nor will I live forever." Aligning one's specific vocation with the vocation of a particular institution is both giving and receiving, extracting and donating to and from generations of people who came before you and will come after you, who, like you, are intelligent and motivated by compassion, by a commitment to excellence, and by an exuberance to serve others that goes way beyond what could ever be accomplished single-handedly by any individual or any single generation.

So, please, keep speaking well of, working hard for, praying for, donating to, and buying from those institutions that dream impossible dreams and aspire to the lofty goal of promoting God's realm on earth. Even though this will not and cannot be realized in any one of our lifetimes, there are plenty of quiet people, the unpretentious faithful, who keep faith despite the fact that cynicism seems more rational, more realistic, more sophisticated, and more cool (as in, insouciantly hip).

You don't have to look very far or live very long to find a multitude of solid reasons to lose faith in humankind, with its seeming mind-lessness. Finding the kind of faith that enables you to see the intrinsic dignity of humans disguised as idiots is more challenging but much more ennobling—and not just for them, but for you and me too. This faith arises when Jesus is the center.

3

LEARNING MORE

*F*reeman Dyson was no neophyte to academia. Before his death in 2020, he taught topics such as theoretical physics for more than fifty years in Princeton, New Jersey. In a 2012 article in the *New York Review of Books*, Dyson noted two enduring institutions in our world: religion and schools.[15] I might add that this especially means religions in which the adherents meet together face-to-face and schools where there are physical campuses requiring tangible human interaction. These sorts of institutions have endured not only because they are grounded in a requisite institutionalism, but also because they accompany their learners with a human factor. Moreover, attentiveness to the human factor ensures room for malleability and adaptivity.

People who get nervous about the introduction of so-called new voices into the curriculum—nervous that it dilutes the strength of Western thought and silences "dead, white males"—may be overestimating the degree to which Western tradition is the same thing as European and underestimating the historical contributions of non-European ideas (e.g., Asian, African, Arabic) to what we call Western. The introduction of variant perspectives from underrepresented communities serves generally to strengthen intellectual thought. Humans are more alike and interconnected (presently and historically) than most of us care

15   Freeman Dyson, "What Can You Really Know?" *New York Review of Books*, November 8, 2012, https://www.nybooks.com/articles/2012/11/08/what-can-you-really-know/.

to admit, and the retreat to ideological enclaves of any sort is often fueled by insecurity, ethnocentric idolatry, and racism.

The systems of rules, rituals, and rote activities serve as a womb of tutelage in which relationships can flourish, where difficult conversations can happen across difference, where even difficult life transitions are embraced as students dare to leave their parents and loved ones (Luke 14:26) and make their way in the world to make a difference. Enduring institutions, in other words, help us to become the more for which we are meant.

It's been some five centuries since the death of Martin Luther. Yet, he was quite ahead of his time regarding the value of education. Four things he said:

1. Luther underscored the liberal arts tradition leading to careers, vocations: "Where are the preachers, jurists, and physicians to come from, if grammar, and other rhetorical arts are not taught?"[6]

2. Educational institutions operated by Christians are avenues of social mobility in which care is demonstrated for the whole person, giving "direction to all temporal estates and offices" and contributing "to the well-being of [people] in body and soul, in property and honor."[7]

3. Governments, he proposed, should support education—especially since governments also rightly support military enterprises, making it mandatory "for the benefit of the whole community."[8]

4. People with wealth should prioritize their charitable giving for education: "Let the rich make their wills with this work in view, as some have done who have established scholar-

---

16   *LW* 46:252.

17   *LW* 46:226, 227.

18   *LW* 46:257.

ship funds." Luther affirmed that God would give "pleasure and joy in Him" to those who engage in educational philanthropy.[19]

When I encounter students who want to quit school, I attempt to have them first ponder two considerations: First, if you're quitting because school is hard, just know that school is hard because it's a part of life, and life is very hard. Dropping out will automatically enroll you in the school of hard knocks, where the grading is less predictable. And second, if you're quitting because your teachers don't inspire you, you have already failed. Find something you love learning about; get curious about it yourself. Don't rely on someone else, such as a teacher. As a famous saying goes, "Education is not the filling of a pail, but the lighting of a fire."

Turning More

The more for which we are meant is often bent by an incapacity or unwillingness to learn. Turning to the Holy Spirit, we discover He's been turned toward us as our teacher and tutor. "But the Helper, the Holy Spirit, whom the Father will send in My name, He will teach you all things and bring to your remembrance all that I have said to you" (John 14:26).

When spurred by the Holy Spirit, the love of learning is sparked by an intellectual curiosity that comes not from a "data dump" of information or an infusion of facts. In fact, Christian intellectuals are not motivated by learning more information, but by learning more about the enigmas of God's universe, the ways of humans, and the mysteries of God. Faith seeks to understand more about the world, the theater of believing. Faith sacrifices privileges, pastimes, and personal pleasures in order to commit to a course of new loves. Faith is more about being formed than being more informed. Faith is about being guided into relationships by wisdom from the hands of One who gently shapes us like "clay in the potter's hand" (Jeremiah 18:6).

---

19 *LW* 46:257.

Faith is about being guided into relationships by wisdom from the hands of One who gently shapes us like "clay in the potter's hand" (Jeremiah 18:6)

My wife, Monique, enjoys trying on makeup as much as purchasing it, particularly at an upscale cosmetics store on 125th Street in New York City. As her dutiful husband, I patiently pass the time by engaging in that spectator sport called people-watching. On one such day, the midsummer Harlem sidewalk, thick with traffic and sticky with humidity, offered me a front-row seat to a dizzying diversity of humanity. I imagined their life stories, none of which were possible to predict or calculate based on their pedestrian, passing appearances.

The sun reappeared finally, but the rain had done its job, cooling the day from blistering city Sahara to a breezily hot sauna. Ponds of water remained on the street. One such pool sat temptingly next to a man perched wearily at the bus stop. He appeared to be a blue-collar worker, like someone who finally punched out to end an irritating day on the job. He rested his body like a sitting duck on the grated ironwork, a makeshift bench, two feet from the puddle. The first curse word left his mouth even before the splash reached him. A parking car zoomed into the puddle, unsettling gritty street water. The driver, oblivious to what he had done, exited the car with a young woman. Seeing him, the drenched gentleman rose to his feet and expressed colorfully his displeasure with the shower he'd just received. "You're a blankety-blank." (Fill in the blanks with expletives.) "Who you talking to?" replied the driver, fortunate to have a wise woman on his arm who tugged him away from a needless confrontation. What came next was instructive, my reward for my patience, and a parable for life. The soaked gentleman returned to exactly the same seat, adjacent to precisely the same puddle, to continue awaiting a bus with larger tires than the car that had already soaked him. Fully armed with a lesson from which he hadn't learned, he returned to the place by the puddle, ready for a second soaking. As he lit a cigarette, I considered approaching him. I pondered chatting with him about what he might have learned from the incident, his anger, his confrontation, his return to the same spot. But I turned back. The same Holy Spirit who gave me the wisdom to exercise caution has a bit more preparatory schooling to do in the life of that brother.

Achieving More

The more for which we are meant is tangible, concrete, and material, not merely spiritual. I agree with Jesus that the real achievers are those who sacrifice pleasure, leisure, and treasure for His sake. Losing your soul for the sake of gaining the whole world is both profitless and pointless (Luke 9:25–26). Happy are the wise who focus on what's good, what's true, and what's beautiful. In our current era, when it seems like baseness, falseness, and ugliness are on the rise, we will look at how the Holy Spirit can work through us for the sake of the life of the world.

"For the peace from above." Those who regularly pray for this peace know it's more than merely a pie-in-the-sky intangible; neither do we get it through the acquisition of things or the achievement of goals. Yes, it comes "from above," but this wholeness also comes "from below" as the community of faith responds holistically to the call of the Holy Spirit. Two of the ways (among many) that it comes to us and through us are when we invest our lives in the curation and redemption of creation and when we work to bring to reality the hopes and the dreams of others. For example, I see peace from above up close and personal as we support our strivers at Concordia College—New York, students who begin to recognize the peace from above as they work their way up from below, who pursue the possibility of social mobility through the promise of education.

In the same way that the word *sign* is tucked into the beginning of the word *significance*, a divine sign always precedes and points us toward our ultimate significance. A sign is something you can see only with the eyes of faith. Similarly, a sign of blessing or a sign of warning is contained within whatever significance in life we might achieve. Too often we get this backward, pursuing significance without being attentive to the Spirit's sign. That's why we don't see—we're too busy chasing stuff that doesn't matter. Exhausted by a chase that leaves us empty, some go through life waggling superficially from job to job, from relationship to relationship, from website to website. Others spin downward into ditches of doubt. I believe the way out is found in, with, and under the font's water and the altar's bread and wine. The font is the place of initiation—a pool or basin—where water is poured on people as God's signature of salvation in the name of the Father, Son, and Holy Spirit. The altar is the table of invitation where all who believe and are baptized receive forgiveness in a sign of restoration and unity. Here, we find Jesus. Here, the eyes of our hearts see the future in new ways—which is why the Lutheran Confessions call these things "signs."[20] Like the Magi who followed the star, faith follows the promise, not counting the costs, the consequences, or the painful crosses that shape us. No, we cannot escape life without scars. Yes, even the best path can be like traveling through a maze in a confused haze, but visible hints show

20   Ap XXIV 69.

up along the journey: signs reminding us of that irrevocable, invisible signature imprinted on our new natures. Do you need reviving today? Mark yourself daily with the sign of the cross, your Baptism. Eat and drink regularly of the gifts at the altar, and then go out into the world without fear. Walk boldly; you've heard the Word! Walk forward as a witness who has sensed the mystically familiar scent of this grace. Significance awaits you in Jesus.

Imagining More

Paint a picture in your mind of who you want to become. Humans possess this rare capability to imagine forward, to think in the hypothetical, to dream creative thoughts, to use the past to think in the present in order to take action for a preferred future. As created co-creators (Genesis 1:26), we exist within a paradox: As created beings, we are limited, but we are also co-creators who have been given dominion over creation to possess creative potential. We are held and beheld by the God who "hangs the earth on nothing" (Job 26:7). We bear the image of God, but we are not, nor shall we ever become, God; so we are not ultimately limitless. We can achieve more only inasmuch as we realize *who* we are and *what* is our relationship with the Creator.

Imagination can be a source of anxiety and fear, or with the Spirit's enlightening, it can be the embryo of creativity and possibility. Anxiety about the future can lead us to yearning for the past. The wise one believes this to be futility. "Say not, 'Why were the former days better than these?' For it is not from wisdom that you ask this" (Ecclesiastes 7:10).

Rather than pining with nostalgia for some golden age of the 1950s, I advocate for Christians to reclaim a confident, cosmic Christology with faith in the fact and act of God loving the whole cosmos (John 3:16) and sending Jesus Christ—the One in whom all things hold together (Colossians 1:17)—to reconcile a fallen creation to the Creator. Our task is to proclaim that truth for the salvation of all who believe the promises. The primal sign of our community is water applied in the name of Father, Son, and Holy Spirit. We gather in Jesus' name at His Table, inviting everyone, since the need for His body and blood for forgiveness applies to everyone and does not exclude anyone. From that altar we are sent, under the influence of the Spirit and with prophetic boldness, to engage the whole world with the same love with which we are loved. We can take this risk because we are confident that Jesus Christ is the "great parenthesis and bracket that unifies the diversity of things."[21]

We resist the reactionary tendency of every era to exaggerate both the urgency of their moment and the enormity of their present challenges. Instead, we are calm, confidently in dialogue with faith and the world as meaning-makers to all, all to the glory of God. Do you doubt that you can live imaginatively in this intersection? Just ask the Holy Spirit, who inhabits past, present, and future.[22]

I am an educator, so one of my favorite roles of Jesus is as *Rabbi*, meaning "teacher." This means Jesus is more than a Savior from sin and our deliverer from self-destruction; He is also a sage master in the way of wisdom. Not only do I delight in watching Jesus as a helper of the helpless, but I also love looking at Him as the One who prepares a pathway for the future, who opens the gateway to opportunities in this life and the next, and who fills our imaginations with what's good, true, beautiful, or possible.

---

21 Arthur Carl Piepkorn, "The One Eucharist for the One World," *Concordia Theological Monthly* 43, no. 2 (February 1972): 100, https://media.ctsfw.edu/Text/ViewDetails/9236.

22 For more on how Christians can take up this important role, see chapter 15, "Communicating More."

4

THINKING MORE

*T*he more for which we are meant is often bent by not recognizing the fact that renewal in our spiritual life also includes transformation by the renewal of our minds (Romans 12:2).

When I was at Valparaiso University, I served on a search committee to hire the new provost and executive vice president for academic affairs. One candidate, Mark Biermann, whom, eventually, we did hire, had a BS, MS, and PhD in optics, that branch of physics dealing with the behavior and quality of light. During interviews, we posed this question: "What does optics have to do with the Lutheran tradition?" This question, of course, was metonymic for a deeper question of relationship between sciences and the humanities.

He smiled and said, "That's a brilliant question." (Which, by the way, I recommend as a tactic when asked arduous questions. It sends self-congratulatory, feel-good endorphins firing through the biologies of the people you want to feel good about hiring you, and it gives the answerer time to think.)

Several seconds later, Biermann replied, "Have you ever heard of Johannes Kepler?"

And since we were all academics, we all nodded as if we had.

"Just in case you hadn't," Biermann continued, "let me refresh your memories. Kepler was a leader in the scientific revolution. He challenged the received orthodoxies up until that time regarding the theory of planetary motion; he suggested that their orbit was not circular—even though God is perfect like a circle—but elliptical. And I believe he had the freedom to challenge what everybody presumed they knew to be true, he had the freedom to innovate, precisely because he was a Lutheran. The faith of Wittenberg encouraged him to turn over the rocks of inquiry, to pursue knowledge, to pursue understanding, and not to worry that if he turned over the rocks of intellectual curiosity some monster lived under that rock who would or could crawl out and gobble up God."

Let's just say from that moment on, he became our benchmark candidate.

Possessing a high IQ is only one piece of the puzzle. It's never only a question of content—knowledge of your doctrine or your curriculum or your political platform. It's almost always also about thinking critically and self-critically with your content, communicating it effectively, showing how it contributes constructively to our life together. Sometimes what we consider rejection of the content has more to do with these. In other words, it could be the way you preach or teach or think too highly about how well you think you think.

Challenging More

Seek truth. Speak truth. Challenge tribal truths with God's transcendent truth. The truth we seek is challenging. Sometimes it feels absurd. Think about these three truths: Jesus is the Son of God, born of a virgin. Jesus, God and man, was crucified and died. Though entirely dead, Jesus arose. This is absurd by human standards, yet as Tertullian puts it, I believe precisely because it's absurd (*credo quia absurdum*).

Mortimer Adler was a student of Aristotle and Thomas Aquinas. He spent a lifetime as a professional philosopher, contemplating the complex realm of ideas. His life and work stretched the expanse of the twentieth century, being born in 1902 and dying in 2001 at age 98. After miles of ink, philosophically trying to make sense of it all—he was not baptized until he was 81 years old—here's what he said about the entanglements of truth: "My chief reason for choosing Christianity was because the mysteries were incomprehensible. What's the point of revelation if we could figure it out ourselves? If it were wholly

MORTIMER ADLER

comprehensible, then it would just be another philosophy."[23] Adler is reverberating an ancient truth from Tertullian's "I believe because it's absurd." In other words, the Christian faith's truth claim of the resurrection makes little human sense. Embrace absurdity, especially the adversity that comes (often unnecessarily and unfairly) when leaning into the absurd dimensions of life. Loving the struggle doesn't mean enjoying the pain; it means being committed to a process that God knows better than we ever can.

It's impossible to literally tell the whole truth. The *whole* truth would derail us with endless details, every concurrent event, every fact in every galaxy everywhere. Only God could know or tell the

---

23   Terry C. Muck, "Truth's Intrepid Ambassador," *Christianity Today*, November 19, 1990, https://www.christianitytoday.com/ct/1990/november-19/profile-truths-intrepid-ambassador.html.

whole truth. If that's our starting point, it begins to make sense why life can feel so absurd, so nonsensical, so irrational, so unreasonable, so un-figure-out-able.

I take great comfort that it's not only I who doesn't get it. The more I live, the more I realize the less I know. With the tip of your finger, tap your chest six times proudly: 1, 2, 3, (rest) 4, 5, 6. Do it again while repeating after me: I / DON'T / KNOW / EV- / ERY- / THING. I often do this with students. Whenever you can both get a laugh and make a point, the greater the odds your teaching will stick. To doubt leads to questions, and questioning leads to learning.

The downside of doubt shows up as a cynicism that can spiral into hopelessness. But healthy doubting leads to questioning, and the questions that arise from authentic reflection lead to faith, despite dire circumstances: "Are You the one who is to come, or shall we look for another?" (Matthew 11:3). I fear false confidence more than my true doubts because cockiness can lead me marching superciliously straight into self-destruction. I have found that questions that cannot be answered are often more important for my spiritual growth than are answers that cannot be questioned.

There is no life that is not encircled by God. There is no person in whom God is not invested. There are no unsupervised processes in the universe. Life is no game of spiritual hide-and-seek. God's love has already found you, and as John 1:16 assures us, all who believe will receive grace upon grace upon grace. "Do I not fill heaven and earth?" says the Lord (see Jeremiah 23:24). Not just the place and time *we* occupy. God is not just our God or the God of just our people or just our nation or our congregation or our denomination or our demographic category or our tribe or ethnicity or language. There is no justice if it's just about us. God is the God of all time and all space and all people. "In [Christ] all things hold together" (Colossians 1:17). I can step into every tomorrow with this fresh recognition that the Holy Spirit wants to fill every nook and cranny of my life until I overflow with God's everlasting love for everybody.

The way of the ancients makes the most sense to me. "Getting it" requires an existential leap, a suspension of rationalism; it demands that we repent from thinking we've got it all figured out. You don't know everything! Live in the mystery. Walk by faith and not by sight.

Forgive the unforgivable. Love the unlovable. See the unseeable and call it blessed.

~~~~~~~~~~~~~~~~~~~~~~~~~~~~~~~~~~~~~

HELP ME, LORD, TO IMPROVE MY SPIRITUAL EYESIGHT AND MY SPIRIT–FORMED INSIGHTS TO LIFE. HELP ME TO SEE THE DIFFERENCE BETWEEN AN OPPORTUNITY AND A TEMPTATION. OPPORTUNITIES FROM YOU LEAD TO BLESSINGS. TEMPTATIONS COME FROM THE WORLD, FROM MY OWN DESIRES, AND FROM THE DEVIL. THESE SOMETIMES FOOL ME, ESPECIALLY AT FIRST, INTO THINKING THEY ARE BLESSINGS. BUT DECISIONS APART FROM YOU LEAD TO TRIALS, TO SUFFERING WITHOUT SOLACE OR SENSE OF DIRECTION. YET, SINCE I AM NAMED FROM ETERNITY AND CLAIMED IN BAPTISM, MY LIFE HAS A GOAL. "I PRESS ON TOWARD THE GOAL FOR THE PRIZE OF THE UPWARD CALL OF GOD IN CHRIST JESUS" (PHILIPPIANS 3:14). WITH GOD'S CALLING ON MY LIFE, THERE IS ALWAYS A WAY OUT OF NO WAY FOR ME, NO MATTER WHAT I'M GOING THROUGH. JESUS IS WITH ME, EVEN IF I CANNOT SEE HIM. HE IS WITH ME—IN, WITH, AND UNDER—IN EVERY CHALLENGE I SEE ALL TOO CLEARLY. GIVE ME THE FAITH TO SEE THIS TRUTH. IN YOUR NAME, I PRAY. AMEN.

~~~~~~~~~~~~~~~~~~~~~~~~~~~~~~~~~~~~~

Mentoring More

I am most certainly a Socratic. I am entirely invested in a question-and-answer, or dialogical, methodology for teaching. Whether it's teaching in the classroom of life or more formally in the academy, I believe that the best learning is like midwifery. The Greeks call this method *maieutic*. The gestation of ideas is brought to birth through the nurturing assistance of mentors.

When teachers, parents, and mentors ask quality questions, it's like they're watering a plant. Children grow when they are engaged with questions that feed the seeds of their imagination, prompt critical thinking, draw them beyond simple assumptions, inspire the fire of curiosity, help them dream about their future. God has placed with us the hearts and minds of young people. Youthful imagination is not the property of young people, and fatigue is not the possession of only the aged. "Even youths shall faint and be weary . . . but they who wait for the LORD shall renew their strength; they shall mount up with wings like eagles; they shall run and not be weary; they shall walk and not faint" (Isaiah 40:30–31).

Whether in ancient, itinerate patterns or in today's high-tech environments, the commitments that faculties and students make to dialogue together also contain commitments to be accountable, be transparent, and relate reliably to one another. Paul's writings show us how the work of informal networks serves the Gospel of Jesus Christ. Silas was a co-worker, co-writer, and co-citizen of Paul and likewise a Jewish citizen of Rome. Silas leveraged his personal relationship with Paul as a passport, gaining him trusty travel passage. Both learners and teachers benefit vitally from these relationships of mutual refreshment (Romans 15:32). Paul and Silas accomplished more together than they could have individually, going "through Syria and Cilicia, strengthening the churches" (Acts 15:41).

Dr. Jerry Kosberg, a coach and counselor to many mentors and protégés, defines a mentor as "somebody who has moved a little further down the road than you have." Mentors know the path, both the theoretical maps and the practical itineraries, along life's journey.

They know the cost of discipleship. They have navigated life's distracting tricks and destructive traps without totally crashing, earning them the right to say to others: "Follow me." That's why Paul dares to offer his own experience as a text of relationship-based instruction: Keep on doing the things "you have learned and received and heard and seen in me" (Philippians 4:9).

In a previous position as the president and CEO of a $50 million, faith-based, international nonprofit, I was privileged to travel the world, to Africa, Asia, and Latin America, to remote and marginalized communities of people living in situations of poverty. In many ways, they are wealthier than we are in the West because of the priority of relationships found in most of these communities. Oral traditions are livelier, storytelling more imaginative, spiritual practices more grounded, learning more holistic. Paul would find himself much more at home there than among us, with our hyperrational, vertical individualism. His language oozed with the priority of relationships and community.

A verse-by-verse sampling of the story of Onesimus in the Book of Philemon reveals an ironic overflow of relational words: "brother," "beloved fellow worker" (v. 1); "sister," "fellow soldier" (v. 2); "I remember you" (v. 4); "your love" (v. 5); "sharing of your faith" (v. 6); "much joy and comfort from your love," "my brother," "refreshed through you" (v. 7); "for love's sake . . . I appeal to you" (v. 9); "my child" (v. 10); "sending him back to you, sending my very heart" (v. 12); "a beloved brother" (v. 16); "your partner" (v. 17); "refresh my heart" (v. 20); "a guest room" (v. 22).

One of the best gifts any mentor has ever given to me was a bit of advice in the form of a mirror. On it (and on my face whenever I look into it) are printed these words: "It's not about you."

In his treatise *The Christian in Society*, Martin Luther wrote that the only way the church can stand, the only way we can stand, is by knowing it's not about us. We must link and stand together and with another Man—the one who linked Himself to us in Baptism and for eternity.

Luther, again, if you don't mind: "For it is another Man who obviously preserves both the church and us."[24]

---

24 *LW* 47:118.

Even though there are times disciples need a difficult word—"exhort and rebuke with all authority," says Paul (Titus 2:15)—mentors can become tormentors when they forget that God is the One who has given them this responsibility. It's not about you! I've carried that mirror and its wisdom with me into every office I've occupied through every transition. While there is a time to lay down the law and call to accountability, authorial positions lose the sharp edge of integrity when they become sledgehammer-like rather than scalpel-like. Authority is for building up, not tearing down (2 Corinthians 10:8).

Mentors accompany their protégés through life's inevitabilities: with support at challenging times, direction through bewildering times, hope for overwhelming times, clarity amid awkward times, and joy in spite of despairing times. The communities they forge are not only family-like as brothers and sisters but also celebrative, leading to multigenerational survival.

Reflecting More

Few events are more celebrative than a graduation. This especially applies to students who are the first in their families to pursue educational opportunity and represents a pathway to social mobility. One particular student caught my attention. At a commencement celebration, the degree she received, a bachelor of arts, suggested that she had acquired a sufficient mastery over certain content. But what suggested that she had *learned* was the mortarboard academic hat she wore that day. This implied humility, critical thinking, self-reflection. Her hat told the world: "I learned how much I still need to learn."

As an icebreaker for a recent event, I posed this question: What's your view of the world in fifty words or less? Here was my answer in forty-two words: "As an educator, I see the world as a classroom where faith is in rigorous pursuit of truth; but since education is also a pathway to new human possibilities, faith grows as it respectfully challenges those who believe they've found the truth." Underlying my answer was the axiom of St. Anselm of Canterbury, *Fides quaerens intellectum*, that is, "faith seeking understanding." Anselm is not attempting to replace faith with understanding or suggest that faith is insufficient without understanding, but that faith or trust in God will seek actively to know more about the One who loves us unreservedly, the God who loves the whole world savingly. Faith knows that we are meant for this more, and living faith actively seeks to know more about God and the world God made. "And it is my prayer that your love may abound more and more, with knowledge and all discernment" (Philippians 1:9).

Learn to lean! To me, that means taking life by the lapels and demanding from it the lessons to be learned. Then, with courageous faith, lean forward and invest your best self for the sake of a future you might not even live to see. Or as someone significantly wiser than I put it: "Trust in the LORD with all your heart, and do not lean on your own understanding. In all your ways acknowledge Him, and He will make straight your paths" (Proverbs 3:5–6).

The verb *reflect* carries the notion that whatever we are reflecting upon is more than what we are able to know, going beyond our own illumination. We reflect the light of another, the One who is the light of the world.

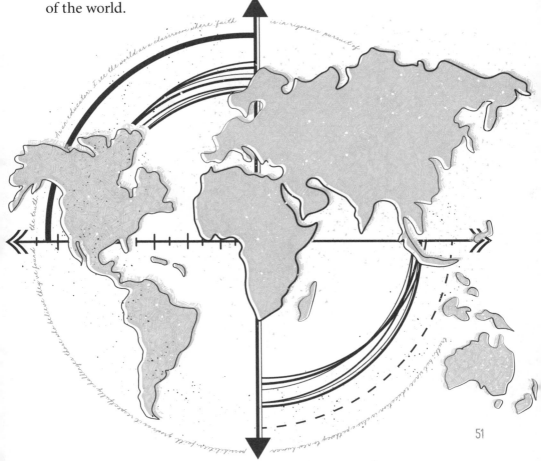

51

5

LOVING MORE

he more for which we are meant is often bent by a loveless-ness that strangulates our lives. That's why it's critical to carefully define our loyalties and our loves. These are the commitments that one day may, in turn, define you. The most critical set of decisions—even more critical than the choice of college or the choice of career—is likely the marital choice of partner for life. Family is the primary arena in which we live out our sense of being meant for more. It's the private training school for public civility.

Desire relates to love in a way that's similar to hunger being related to being healthy. If you're never hungry, you won't ever eat, and if you don't eat, you won't ever be healthy. Hunger can be a starting state for healthiness, and desire can drive one to want to be (or remain) in a relationship with someone, but too many people confuse that desire with real, relational love. Neither hunger as healthiness nor desire as love are to be confusingly equated.

People are seeking true love. It's not easy to find love in our twenty-first-century social media world of Fakebook and Crapchat, with our instantaneously Instagrammable lives lived at a dizzying, digitized pace that places a premium on externals, appearance, material investments, and sexual attractiveness, confusing all of that with real love. People are seeking love and are met by meanness in the form of slapdash memes that are meant to be humorous but are cowardly cheap shots that ridicule others for a laugh. Cruel schoolyard teasing is evinced.

People are seeking true love. I'm not sure I understand that phrase, but I do believe that true love is not something you find in the finding of another person. When two people "find" one another, it's the next two steps that make the marriage. The first step is committing to see your life as a part of something bigger than yourselves: the institution of marriage is the spinal column of a strong society; people are counting on you and praying for you to stay married. The second is committing to seek the help you need from God's Word, marital mentors, and counseling. Any marriage that makes it out of the honeymoon phase is proof of God's merciful protection.

True love is something you create, not something you find or that finds you, not something you fall into. True love will require more forgiveness from you than you ever thought possible. I believe that our deepest longings are not satisfied when we pursue them directly. Satisfaction for those things we most deeply desire comes as a by-product of delighting ourselves in the Lord (Psalm 37:4). As we delight ourselves in the gifts of God, we learn how our needs and longings are fed and how our energy is fueled to turn outward in love toward others. "Here your heart must go out in love and learn that this is a sacrament of love."[25] You are loved and supported in the Sacrament. Go out to love and support those who need it. This is why we need to eat and drink more of the blessed Sacrament of the body and blood of Jesus Christ.

Professional counseling is helpful. My preference is for skilled guides with a seasoned Christian worldview. Bookstore shelves are sometimes filled with the pop psychology of oversimplistic solutions. In our therapeutic culture, there are many psychological approaches to overcoming hatred. These are intended to be helpful and advanced as proven but can become trendy, like a faddish "hate loss" diet. Jesus Christ offers the surest cure for the unforgiveness that afflicts us. It's lengthy, but consider it a feast, an ancient formula:

> Let love be genuine. Abhor what is evil; hold fast to what is good. Love one another with brotherly affection. Outdo one another in showing honor. Do not be slothful in zeal, be fervent in spirit, serve the Lord. Rejoice in hope, be patient in tribulation, be

---

25 *LW* 35:54.

constant in prayer. Contribute to the needs of the saints and seek to show hospitality.

Bless those who persecute you; bless and do not curse them. Rejoice with those who rejoice, weep with those who weep. Live in harmony with one another. Do not be haughty, but associate with the lowly. Never be wise in your own sight. Repay no one evil for evil, but give thought to do what is honorable in the sight of all. If possible, so far as it depends on you, live peaceably with all. Beloved, never avenge yourselves, but leave it to the wrath of God, for it is written, "Vengeance is Mine, I will repay, says the Lord." To the contrary, "if your enemy is hungry, feed him; if he is thirsty, give him something to drink; for by so doing you will heap burning coals on his head." Do not be overcome by evil, but overcome evil with good. (Romans 12:9–21)

We are loved beyond what our brains can contain (Ephesians 3:19), loved by a lover whose unlimited love hung on the cross for you, and in this crucified and resurrected Jesus all things hang together (Colossians 1:17)! We might sometimes feel fragile, fried, like life is fraying, like we're running on empty. But our pain is not without purpose, because we are filled with the fullness of God so that we can witness from our weakness and so that we can pour out ourselves for others (Philippians 2:17). As Jeremiah found out, you cannot out-pour-out God. The pessimist thinks, "My cup is half empty." The optimist thinks, "My cup is half full." We believe with the psalmist that "my cup overflows" because there is nowhere that God's love is not!

WE are LOVED BEYOND what our BRAINS CAN CONTAIN (EPHESIANS 3:19)

Forgiving More

Forgiving others can be just as difficult as forgiving ourselves. To look repeatedly on that tyrannical parade of life's what-ifs will drive you to drink, to madness, or—if you allow yourself to be drawn forward by the grace of God—to some previously unconsidered possibilities offered uniquely in the fresh forgiveness of Jesus. This last pathway makes possible a high ground to healthiness in your soul, regardless of the things you've done, said, and thought, or failed to do, say, or think. While selectively remembering our past can deliver us from the insanity of regret, it also can lead us to a worse place: the opposite insanity of sanitized, arrogant self-righteousness. Such editing of our abuses, our "issues," our crimes, and our peccadilloes happens in individuals, families, communities, societies, or nations. Sin (the biblical term for the stuff we've done or left undone) is not only personal but also structural. The healthier, even holier, approach to our messed-up histories is to own them, face them, embrace them, grace them with forgiveness, learn from them, wash them in the blood-bought promises of Jesus, cast them on His cross, get over them, and get on with life.

Martin Luther's reformation of the church was sparked in part because he felt like he wasn't good enough, wasn't righteous enough, hadn't done enough to earn God's acceptance. He finally located that acceptance in Romans 1:17. God knows how we want and, more important, how we savingly *need* to be loved, and God pulls off this love in Jesus Christ.

God's requirement is that we should love *loving kindness*, the English translation of the Hebrew word *chesed* (see Micah 6:8). This word, *chesed*, carries a covenantal quality; it's a deeply relational term, linguistically and theologically related to the sense of "steadfast love" and "mercy" and to the juridical terms *justice* and *forgiveness*, being abundant in pity-heartedness (see Exodus 34:6–7).

So, what are the risks in choosing to approach life's problems with power-game solutions, steamrolling over others and backstabbing those who get in the way? Since, as Luther says, "everyone desires to sit at the head of the group and to be seen before all" rather than be in service to God and others, we easily can be tempted into bypassing pathways to peacemaking for the sake of unprincipled human victories.[26] Two risks come to mind, two reasons God may have commanded us to avoid the anger and impatience that lead to combat instead of conciliation: (1) If the only rule we abide by is survival of the fittest, eventually everyone will get crushed, including you. (2) Any temporary victory you finagle will be of the sort Jesus warns against, winning the world but losing your soul (Mark 8:36). Why losing your soul? Because acts of vengeance might give you a temporary vindication, as if you were winning the world, but they also serve to self-destructively harden your soul. And once a soul is calcified, it becomes difficult for grace to penetrate, for mercy to infiltrate, for forgiveness to be appropriated when Jesus arrives.

Chesed is one of the most beautiful Hebrew words in both its sound and in what it signifies. *Chesed* finds its fullness in the divine character, bursting forth with a doxological pleroma of forgiveness (Micah 7:18–20): "Who is a God like You?" Not miserly with *misericordia* (mercy) but pardoning offenses, commuting sentences, suspending punishments, extending new leases on life, passing over faults, drowning sin like the Egyptians (a baptismal foreshadowing), showing a unique faithfulness that leads to complete forgiveness. Now, with this final form of justice cross-marked on our Christ-anointed faces as forgiveness, we begin to walk humbly with our God and learn to walk a straight mile, doing justice and loving mercy.

There are multiple ways to be in an unhealthy relationship with the past, but one significant way is to never get beyond a past grievance, never to heal from a historical hurt. I think about African American slavery and Jim Crow, about Native American dispossession, about Tutsis slaughtering Hutus, Turks slaughtering Armenians, and the Protestant/Catholic battles in Northern Ireland. Letting go does not deny the pain, but provides an avenue to healing. Not letting go steals from your strength and hope for tomorrow; it eclipses potential. Don't resign yourself to live in that sort of rut.

Consider these four incentives to forgive others:

---

26   LC III 103.

1. I've been forgiven much.

2. Life is too short for unforgiveness.

3. I am meant for more than the brutal captivity of resentment.

4. My future possibilities deteriorate when I'm focused on past negatives with people, in places, or at events.

Some Christians seem to perpetuate a theological fiction about coupled togetherness; simply put, not everyone is meant to be married. After Adam and Eve took the fatal bite that caused them to lose their Eden, the scriptural examples are scarce of the sort of marriage we stylize in Western culture as the "biblical family." There is neither a need to punish oneself for choosing singleness nor a need to remain mired in guilt or shame because of marital failure. By grace, any blood on your hands has been, by Christ's blood, erased.

Do we dare to try at marriage again? Do we dare to try this at all? Do we dare tread previously untrodden roads? God's forgiveness, given to us fully and freely in Jesus Christ, gives us the freedom to dare unconsidered possibilities as we imagine in the Spirit new futures of faithfulness. Can we create a life together even though less than half of families are two-parent households in their first marriage? The odds are against us, but are we willing to make the sacrifice that it takes in order to reap the reward of the more that marriage gives, the more made possible only by a love as real as life, and by a forgiveness as alive as the resurrected Jesus?

Consider this passage: "Christ Jesus is the one who died—more than that, who was raised—who is at the right hand of God, who indeed is interceding for us" (Roman 8:34). When Luther saw these words, he applied them to the sacrificial feast of love at the altar: "From these words we learn that we do not offer Christ as a sacrifice, but that Christ offers us. And in this way it is permissible, yes, profitable, to call the mass a sacrifice; not on its own account, but because we offer ourselves as a sacrifice along with Christ."[27] Purchased by the victory

---

27   *LW* 35:99.

of the atoning sacrifice of Jesus, we in turn are offered sacrificially by that same Jesus Christ for the life of the world.

Absorbing More

So many aspects of being a college president—and before that, frankly, the president and CEO of an international nonprofit—are secular in character: legal matters, human resources issues, budgetary challenges, fund-raising. By "secular," I mean a direct distinction with my pastoral vocation is delineated. That's why I find it curious that colleagues and friends persist in turning to me to ask questions that relate to pastoral theology. A version of one of those is "I know there is evil in the world, but I had hoped that goodness outweighed the bad. Apparently, it does not! What's your take, pastor-president?"

One of my favorite theology professors, E. Edward Hackmann, once taught us: "Never be shocked at the depths of human depravity which will often unravel before your eyes. Treat all people with God-given dignity, as if you hope for more, but don't be surprised when they don't live up to it." Sadly, his cautionary instruction has served me impeccably over decades—not only in dealing with others but with myself as well. The human condition is perfectly situated for forgiveness.

In an attempt to boost ratings and raise profits, both mainstream media and social media tend to oversimplify arguments and exaggerate stories. This serves their primary mandate as publicly traded companies to be responsive to shareholder investments. That priority may even soften their willingness to tolerate recklessly lopsided arguments from semi-informed, rage-driven flame-throwers fuming with comments that attract eyeballs and generate likes but don't do too much to promote love for neighbor or the social media company's community-building goals. We are meant for more than mere verbosity with increasing intensity. "The more words, the more vanity," observes Solomon, "and what is the advantage" to humanity (Ecclesiastes 6:11)? We are meant for the love with which we are loved by God to "abound more and more" (Philippians 1:9).

6

DIVERSIFYING MORE

*O*ver twenty years ago, I wrote a book in which I explored the question "Is *diversity* a dirty word?" I developed answers to questions I had grappled with for a quarter of a century, and some of those answers I now disavow. In this life, the enlightening work of the Spirit is always inchoate. However, one topic in that volume from 1999 remains as germane as ever: diversity. Then, I attempted to address the highly charged distinctions and frustrating divisions between people groups. I suggested, and I still maintain, that these intercultural questions constitute a "deep, discerning, and thoughtful exercise, one that is never rushed into and never finished."[28] The dynamism of cultural interpretation, especially as juxtaposed with the dynamic work of God's enlightening Spirit, remains unfinished. God's goal for humanity consists of a Christian pluralism, namely, interacting positively with different individuals or groups without spiraling into factionalism.

I maintain that we are meant for way more than mere maintenance, and the more we let the Spirit open our eyes to recognize what's missing and what's amiss in a world like this, the more we ourselves will realize the mission meant for our own lives.

---

28 John Nunes, *Voices from the City: Issues and Images of Urban Preaching* (St. Louis: Concordia Publishing House, 1999), 54.

A Calamity in the Shop

There is a barbershop I frequent in Yonkers, New York. It's a global place. Many ethnicities and languages are represented—Dominicans, Nigerians, White European-Americans, Puerto Ricans, Jamaicans, Hondurans, African Americans, a variety of Asians—and many rhythmic music styles, including hip-hop, reggaeton, merengue. It's loud and lively; the typical fashion here is urbanwear. Conversations range from sports to relationships, spiced with jesting, verbal jostling, and joking. Colorful language is not unfamiliar parlance—especially when women and children aren't present.

Then, one of the barbers, a motorcyclist in his twenties, was killed in a hit-and-run accident. The shop went silent. It became churchlike.

A shrine was set up where his barber chair was, draped in black. For several weeks, no music played. A candlelight vigil was held one evening with open wailing and rivers of tears. Prayerlike calls for justice arose. Offerings were taken to support the next of kin. The ritual trappings and quasi-liturgical trimmings of spirituality pervaded the space. I admired how the reverential responses were motivated by a restless quest for the sacred, for answers from something beyond this world. The instinct was right. They were reaching for some sign of spirituality, some symbol of the holy, but most were deeply unsatisfied by the situation, unable to find anything much to quench the restlessness. Their anger rose at the unjust circumstances of the accident that killed their friend. There was plenty of outward raving but not much inward satisfaction (2 Timothy 3:5). The *more* seemed beyond reach. Within months, life basically returned to normal.

Sixteen hundred years ago, St. Augustine suggested that this was the normal state for humans. We naturally know we are made for more, meant for more, and our hearts are on a restless edge until this dilemma is resolved.

My hope for my students, my colleagues, and my barbershop friends alike is that they will be positively provoked to exercise eye-opening discernment. I define this as the process of coming to know more profoundly and think more deeply about what they are seeing in their day-to-day lives, rather than just seeing what they think they've already come to know. For it is "in, with, and under" the ordinary things that the presence and promises of God are implanted.

Augustine's truth is timeless: restlessness remains our lot until we land in the land of ultimacy and soul-satisfaction, union with God forever. What we call death on earth is known by Christians, *sub cruce* (under the cross), to be life.

New life in Christ is a once-for-all event. We are saved like a punctuation mark. It happens in Jesus' bloody execution on a cross, is imprinted on every individual's watery death to sin in Baptism, and is seized by every believer who by faith receives the free grace of God. While the payment for sin is death, the promise of Christ's work has benefits for this life and the next (John 10:10; Romans 6:23): Jesus' sacrificial death and victorious resurrection is for us! Theologically speaking, this is seamless, simultaneous, and instantaneous. Life in the Spirit and the enjoyment of salvation's surplus, on the other hand, represent an eye-opening process, or as the catechism puts it, the Holy Spirit works through Word and Sacraments to "enlighten" us—which in Luther's German literally means "to turn on the light."

The more we walk in God's Word, the more we come to know God's will in, with, and under our day-to-day lives. This means we build relationships we never thought possible with people we never previously considered in our circle. I believe we should begin simply with a confidence in God's transcendent truth, which erases the tribal truths that kick some people out, keep certain people down, divide people up, and box people into categories (Ephesians 2:14). The mirages of division are eliminated by divine love; in the judgment of transcendent truth, categories like race are at best nonexistent and at worst flawed.

Tribal Truths vs. Transcendent Truth

However, because too many people, including Christians, are falsely convinced of their own ethnic group's tribal truths, racism remains a stingingly oppressive reality. There are no reputable scientists or credible theologians who would acknowledge race as an essential category for distinguishing humans. Yet, the record of history, socioeconomics, politics, and power categorically shows that the consequences of racism cannot be denied.

When will we, especially those of us in Christ's Church who claim a theology of transcendent truth, not only claim our own status as created in the image of God but also extend that dignity to all people—even to those who don't walk like us or talk like us or play like us or pray like us? I believe that all humans derive from the same Creator. All are offered Jesus' saving love. And even in dealing with those who refuse that gracious invitation, all Christians are called by the Spirit to be leaders in treating all others as if our common humanity is more enduring (which it is) than our petty, murderous, sin-soaked tribal truths.

Holding to the justice of transcendent truth does not preclude holding individuals accountable for their actions or responsible for their ideologies. No one gets off the hook just because he or she possesses inherent dignity. On the contrary, we must challenge those whose tribal truths fan the flames of racism and Islamophobia, which contribute to the evil we saw at the Emanuel African Methodist Episcopal Church shooting in 2015 or to the 2019 massacre at two mosques in, of all places, Christchurch, New Zealand.

Real Righteousness

Compared to the way the world works, Christianity is upside-down and inside-out. Few things remind us of this more than the transcendent truth of the incarnation, the enfleshment of God in Jesus Christ. This truth scrapes against the pseudo-self-righteousness and trivial tribalism that cleave humanity. This truth challenges us to be unafraid of being different or dealing with difference. Our faith is not worldly, but it is essentially catholic, global, and intercultural; therefore, we strive for real diversity. The way of the world prefers unity of thought and uniformity of behavior—associating only with people who walk like us, talk like us, look like us, cook food like us, dance (or can't dance) like us. Sameness seems so much easier. But don't get it twisted—preserving a lack of diversity also takes work. Screening. Weeding out. Shunning. Dismissing. Dissing. Resisting the Spirit. My point is our lack of difference is rarely incidental, random, or because of that age-old excuse "We just want the most qualified candidates."

I see this absence of diversity happening across the ideological spectrum. Without divine prompting, all groups tend to drift into the calming reassurance of an uncomplicated homogeneity. Cue a tableful of heads nodding in prosaic sycophancy. It's a self-reinforcing circle of yeses. We've seen, either tacitly or with the pride of a parade, that all-too-easy moment when groups congratulate their fellow members on the superiority of their virtue (especially when contrasting our supposed virtuosity with those who are deemed to be demonically deluded or irrationally deceived; ironically, they are no less dug-in in their opinions than we are).

A lack of diversity, that vain pursuit of purity of perspective, is sometimes a reflection of being so insecure that we can't threaten the remaining thin thread of security we have left by even listening to an outsider. Of course, according to both natural law and the US Constitution, for example, your right to your perspective is not as protected as, say, your right to life and liberty. But if we were as secure as we claim, we would be more open to dialogue.

That's because unless we daily make the sign of the cross and remind ourselves that we're made in the image of God and remade in the image of Christ, the common default is a distorted self-image, an incurvature of the ego. The natural self tends to "fear the mirror"—that is, there's something about us we so deeply detest that we double down to protect ourselves from human reminders of that trait. Perpetrators of distorted confidence major in masquerading, in what Luther called "self-styled" righteousness,[29] marshaling their appearance to maintain the status quo, to impress the crowd. There's not much room for meaningful diversity when we're committed to compensatory grandiosity.

Real righteousness, on the other hand, always shakes things up. Real power always stirs up the normalcy of complacent indecency. Real hope is always alien. Real community dares dangerously to embrace both Alpha and Omega, as well as every unlettered exception in between. Real salvation always breaks in from the outside as a stranger. God's love both creates faith and anchors it in a confidence that enables action.

---

29   *LW* 24:177.

Real love flows from the faith that I am unshakably loved, which is why I am really able to love even my persecutors. "From heaven above to earth I come," one hymn puts it, knowing in advance the dangers and the blessings this earthly journey would bring—and that, my friends, is the epitome of being upside-down and inside-out.

More of Us!

When I say we need more of us and less of them, I don't mean that we need more people who walk, talk, look, cook, dance, or vote like us. Rather, I mean that we need to include more people who are *not* like us in the category we call "us."

That's why the following two phrases are pet peeves of mine: "they just don't get it" and "they just need to get over it." I find these two phrases divisive and dismissive. Both sentences begin with that most mischievous of pronouns, *they*. This word usage parades with cocky ambiguity. It pushes unique individuals into nondescript piles of humanity, making them conveniently dismissible. But this pronoun also conceals a dagger of specificity suggesting that *they* ("the problem") are not like *us* ("the enlightened").

The first phrase ("they just don't get it") refers to some plain fact that others either don't or can't comprehend, while the second phrase ("they just need to get over it") refers to some fact of past pain or belief from which others need to recover. Our greater work is empathy, struggling to understand the world of others. For example, Jesus showed mercy to people whom He compassionately regarded as harassed and helpless. He didn't belittle or dismiss them but felt deeply for those suffering from a leadership deficit, lost like shepherdless sheep (Matthew 13). Whenever we jump to the tidy explanation that "they just don't get it" or "they just need to get over it," we take the fast track away from relationships and toward the dead end of simpleminded analysis—as evidenced by the second word in each phrase, *just*. *Just* comforts us with a lazy illusion of simplicity.

Indeed, there are facts we'd prefer people to "get" and matters that we'd have others "get over." But demanding this in a degrading way does the opposite: building walls and wedges where we need bridges and avenues of understanding. Neither phrase serves those against whom it is used and instead permits those using the phrase to justify their stance, minimize their responsibility, and raise the level of loyalty and zealotry in their own circles. Neither phrase does much good when you're trying—especially in times of change—to build a cohesive community, grow an organization, or do God's changeless work in this ever-changing world.

No matter where you are on the political, economic, or spiritual spectrum, "getting it" and "getting over it" are more likely to happen in relationships of we than in constructions of us versus them.

7

EMPTYING MORE

*T*he path to the more for which we are meant does not happen without a sense of service for one another. Jesus "emptied Himself, by taking the form of a servant, being born in [human] likeness" (Philippians 2:7).

Living in tribes helps keep us alive. It's easier to identify a potential enemy. It's simpler to tell who's an ally and who's a threat to my survival. The tribal instincts of humans that, on the positive side, contribute to keeping us alive, are in our time more alive with full force, red-hot tribalism. We defend our mounds of dust, of dirt, of stuff without significance. We gobble up grotesque, extreme stories in pixelated distortions of one another; even believers can quickly forget the ultimate death we've already died to ourselves, to our traditionalism, and to our tribalism: the death with Jesus from which we're raised as martyrs, confident, risking freely every other death in pursuit of both peace and justice. Few risk emptying themselves for the sake of the other, for the happy exchange in seeing others gain an advantage.

The God-instinct of transcendent truth is against the human instinct of tribal truth. Because of it, Jesus placed Himself into our human condition, emptying Himself, humbling Himself, putting Himself in a position of servitude for our sake. I call this the ultimate act of humanitarianism: when God became human for our sake. Martin Luther called this a happy exchange (*der fröhliche Wechsel*). We get the saving health that comes from the God who takes on, in a divine trade-off, our sin-sickness.

Majority "Minority"

It's always struck me as ironic that something like 85 percent of the world's population qualifies as "minority" depending on how you count. Obviously, this term refers more to power dynamics than numerical demographics. Because of this, I have an academic friend who uses the term *minoritized*—referring to groups of people who have been made into minorities. I believe that our faith calls us to reject such differentiating of people and to actively, intentionally resist it. I further believe that race as a category doesn't really exist, yet racism is real.

That's why we must work with intentionality. I tend to oppose the use of quotas to achieve diversity. Too often they turn people into objects and reduce them to superficial categories; what's more, their arbitrariness reinforces the natural resistance all humans have to differences. All that said, people who claim they want more diversity but just can't find "qualified minorities" might have a bigger problem, namely, a narrow-mindedness that sabotages their own success. My experience is that the qualities of a so-called minority perspective serve as their own unique qualifier. In other words, intentionally selecting talented communicators from underrepresented communities will bring to the table points of view that will likely modify your menu of what qualifies as a qualification; are additive and, even when difficult to hear, more problematic when left unheard; and will help your organization adapt to demographic shifts.

Even though most of the ways we are divided from one another are fictional categories that don't really exist biologically or theologically, discrimination is yet a sinful fact of life. Various forms of supremacy rage around us like a roaring lion behind the sin-filled covers of false power and false glory. Especially in our times, it seems like we are witnessing what the ancient prophet Isaiah calls a rise among those "who call evil good and good evil, . . . who acquit the guilty for a bribe, and deprive the innocent of [their] rights" (Isaiah 5:20, 23). As sheep of the Good Shepherd sent into a wolfish, dog-eat-dog world, we are commanded by Jesus (Matthew 10:16) to be "wise as serpents" about the realities such as discrimination and the dangerous ideologies that threaten all that's good and true and beautiful. Paranoia is unhelpful, but sober-minded watchfulness (1 Peter 5:8) seems more critical than ever. Yes, we better stay woke! But don't let that stop us from praying with hope and working with positivity.

In our wisdom, awareness, and circumspection, we must not spiral into a hard-hearted paranoia or a cold-blooded cynicism. Jesus invites us to be as "innocent as doves," building peace bridges constructed in the name of the One whose death and resurrection has already broken down all the lame excuses people muster up for human divisions.

Even when the grave seems to conquer, when evil seems to triumph, the reality of Easter still stands. Like Christ on both Palm Sunday and Resurrection Sunday, we rise above the noisemaking, political grandstanding, social-media showboating, fearmongering. We rise as peacemakers, bridge-builders, hope-dealers, quick to listen and slow to speak, confessing concretely the resurrection insurrection: Christ is risen indeed. Alleluia.

Not for Lutherans Only | PART 2

While "ethnic, social, and sexual identities do not determine one's standing before God," there's no arguing that the "distinctions [that are] present in creation remain."[30] A question for us might be how does our theological tradition guide us practically regarding this diversity? On one hand, differences enhance life with stylistic variety, differentiated functioning, and cultural "spice." On the other hand, in our sin-devastated world, differences can become occasions for painful division and negative discrimination. Sadly, in this latter regard, even Christians have room to grow—including North American Lutherans. Two points for us to consider:

1. Christians in the Lutheran tradition tend to have strengths and weaknesses when it comes to disciple making. Our strength is the *how* of the Gospel's "Go, make disciples"—by baptizing and teaching. Our tradition tends to comprehend

---

30 *The Lutheran Study Bible*, note on Galatians 3:28.

and confess well the refined sacramental practices and clearly defined doctrines of the Word that create and sustain faith. Our weakness tends to be the *to whom* of "Go, make disciples"; we struggle to reach out to "all people," especially people who don't share our ethnic, social, or sexual identity. Lutherans are more white and English-speaking than any other religious group in North America.[31]

2. Keeping that in mind, we should resist the temptation to be so talkative about the *how*—our strength—and pray for the Holy Spirit's patience to listen more to and learn more from those who compose anthropologically the *to whom*—our weakness. By taking seriously all people (not just those whom we select out and parade around as our preferred exceptions from among those who are not like us), we would do a better job at disciple making. Our goal should be to permit our strength (the *how*) to be informed by diverse voices (the *to whom*) and thus strengthen our faithfulness in following the command of Jesus in Matthew 28.

We are called to be allies and advocates for those with intellectual difficulties, those whom too many in our world consider disposable. Too many people disappear behind their titles or their tribes or their shortcomings. We are losing fellow travelers created in God's image who disappear behind an image that is not eternal, nonessential, and cannot save them.

Our core identity as baptized believers matters more than any label: professor, conservative, parent, steelworker, Latina, computer programmer, progressive, bishop, or learning disabled. What God does for us in three splashes of water is bigger than the pigeonholes in which we put ourselves.

In one way or another, each of us struggles, teetering on the edge, one slip from being lost. More critically, we are all the lesser because of those we've lost along life's way. Think about your loved ones who are

---

31   Michael Lipka, "The Most and Least Racially Diverse U.S. Religious Groups," Pew Research Center, July 27, 2015, http://pewrsr.ch/1KtFGxx.

lost in some aspect of life. You realize you are lesser because of it. Any lackluster concern we have for those who are lost reveals a lack of love.

We should particularly care about those who are lost in a way that *appears* to be alive, but whose humanity, who they really are, has all but totally disappeared behind a title or a tribe or a shortcoming. That's the point. There is no propositional language with which we can rescue the lost, no catchphrase, no formulaic truth that will remove the veil from their eyes and enable them to find their way. God "desires all people to be saved and to come to the knowledge of the truth" (1 Timothy 2:4).

A shortcoming of religion is the temerarious evangelism of the well-intended that bludgeons "the lost" into numbness with calls to action for which they are not one iota motivated nor have an inkling of faith to do. The Law always accuses, and without faith, the Law does not lead to anything good. The Law does not create faith; only the Gospel does. By faith, the faithful can do good works, which show up in love for the lost.

Be the love the people you call "lost" need. Be the love that will draw them to faith. The Word of God always comes first. "After it follows faith; after faith, love; then love does every good work, for . . . it is the fulfilling of the law."[32] The action of God working through the faithful doing deeds of love precedes the drawing of the lost to saving faith in Jesus. Our work is to love them freely and cheerfully, not to place demands on them that they cannot understand and that they experience primarily as onerous on their part and self-righteous on our part. Invite your neighbors into our parade.

The Jesus March

I imagine Jesus struggled with the expectations of the fiesta-goers on the first Palm Sunday, which is why He chose for His Jesus-mobile an unceremonious colt—the equivalent of a used Ford Fiesta without a chauffeur instead of a limo. I imagine He struggled with how people are so tempted by the supposed largeness of titles, such suckers for empty spectacles of show-offery (although Jesus probably never said

---

32   *LW* 36:39.

"suckers," and "show-offery" is not a word). The crowds crowned Jesus with glory and honor. Some zealots attempted to co-opt the Jesus march for their agenda. You can almost see it in their eyes . . . the celebration of relief. They're quite rightly fed up with being occupied by Roman colonialist rule, so as they pin their political hopes on Jesus, they are ecstatic, hands in the air, palms waving like they just don't care, shouting bloodthirstily until they're hoarse with veins popping in their necks, "Surely, this is the One we've been waiting on to bring in our empire, our power, our glory right here from Jerusalem, forever and ever. Hosanna! Amen."

And while Jesus never denies the accolades, never refutes their cheers, never shushes the crowds ("Oh, no, please, stop, you don't get it!"), in His eyes, we see something haunting, a mysterious foreshadowing of the cross. The trajectory for Holy Week, frankly, is downhill, especially for power brokers! Jesus empties Himself. Rather than disappearing behind a title or tribe or shortcoming, Jesus models an opposite move. Jesus takes His title, His divinity, His tribe, the fullness of the Trinity and hides His deity behind His human identity.

Rather than Jesus going up to the center of Jerusalem dripping with Hosannas, I imagine Him undistracted by the noise, taking this march in a direction nobody expected, angling first toward a garden, Gethsemane, and then toward the margins, the edges, toward that godforsaken place of outcasts and common criminals—that's where Jesus takes the march for you and for me.

If you feel like an outsider, Jesus comes for you. If you feel unforgivable, like there's nothing you can do to get your life back on track, Jesus comes for you. Martin Luther offers some color commentary on what Jesus is up to: "This King does not rule by means of money, possessions, and external devices [or power]"; He is nonetheless a ruler like none other, who "can save and help where no man, no creature on earth or in heaven can help—against sin, that we may not be damned by it; against death, that it may not devour us; against the devil, that he may not keep us captive."[33]

Jesus hides His power and glory behind His humanity so that we are not damned by our reckless pursuits of power and glory, nor devoured

---

33 *LW* 13:239.

by our insatiable need to be highly regarded, nor captive to spending a lifetime making a name for ourselves.

Jesus hides His power and glory behind His humanity to die on our behalf so that those who join the Jesus march can die to themselves; so that we are not damned to selling our souls in order to gain a bit of prestige in our own Jerusalem or Athens, nor devoured by our own pride-fueled ambitions, nor captive to the inflated images of ourselves that never allow any room for others to get in.

Jesus hides His power and glory behind His humanity so that we are not damned because of our diverse human identities, nor devoured by haters who love to hate, nor captive to our own thirst for revenge so real we can taste it.

Jesus hides His power and glory behind His humanity so that the Holy Spirit can come down Sunday after Sunday and imprint God's power and God's glory on us, through Word and water and bread and wine, investing us with the one identity that we cannot screw up—well, we can and do screw it up, but not in any permanent way. Thank You, Jesus, for inviting us to join a march that transcends title or tribe or shortcoming.

Here's the deal: Jesus, the ultimate humanitarian, gives more in order to take away more of what keeps us from being the more for which we are meant. Jesus Christ is our hope. He is the One who "has broken down in His flesh the dividing wall of hostility" (Ephesians 2:14). Jesus does this with an in-the-flesh investment for us, a blood, sweat, and tears commitment for our salvation, a protoplasmic down payment for every human person ever born. We who are born again are meant for more.

If you feel like an outsider, Jesus comes for you. If you feel unforgivable, like there's nothing you can do to get your life back on track, Jesus comes for you.

8

TRANSFIGURING MORE

orders and Boundaries." These riveting words served as the theme for a recent academic year at Concordia College—New York. As a Christian higher education community, we are learning about what we see in the world around us:

- The borders being passionately fought over in political news

- The ravages of boundaries being violated as seen in the #MeToo movement

- The biological and technological borders being crossed and creating ethical quandaries, especially at the boundary of life and death

- The theological borders and cultural boundaries dividing Christians from one another in denominations

- The healthy boundaries and necessary borders that keep us safe and keep order in society

"The lines have fallen for me in pleasant places" (Psalm 16:6). Here, the psalmist gives thanks for his life, for the goodness that has encompassed his existence, ordered his steps, and bordered his livelihood with flourishing. Why God chooses to do a certain thing among a certain people in a certain place is largely uncertain to us. There are so many mysteries that cannot be seen. Two millennia ago,

Jesus Christ assumed a boundaried existence, entering a short slice of human history at the eastern end of the Mediterranean Sea. From His birth in a spare barn to His degrading death on a crude cross, He lived within the borders of the same human traumas and trials that we endure. In His crucified flesh, He broke down the "dividing wall of hostility" between us (Ephesians 2:14)—those divisive borders that keep us from seeing our salvation. He also transcends and transfigures all things, encompassing all time and time zones, all borders and boundaries, all spaces and places, all nations and races, and rendering them meaningless within the scope of eternity.

The Disrupter

Jesus came as a disrupter. The Rev. Dr. Alberto García, a relentless scholar, completed a translation from Latin to Spanish of Martin Luther's commentary of the prophet Micah. He suggested to me that, in one verse of that book of the Bible, the best English translation for Jesus Christ is what Luther calls "the disrupter," the One who interrupts the flow of things in this life.[34] We, too, are called to be disrupters in Jesus' name. In an upside-down world, in a world with topsy-turvy values and perverted priorities, in a world that in so many ways is heading in the wrong direction, God is calling us to savingly disrupt the patterns of this world. We can do this by being humble, rather than cockily proud, in our conversations about our faith (1 Peter 3:15).

Even the way God gathers that flock we call the church is disruptive, despite how relatively homogenous many churches are. Look around at all the strangely beautiful or beautifully strange but indeed different kinds of people whom God gathers: the diversity of the sheep, the mediocrity of the other sheep, not us, of course. The amount of repair work and forgiveness they need, their certain failure as candidates to be saints, their messed-up families and even worse family secrets.

God calls especially those who recognize their unworthiness, those who desire Christ's healing love and mercy that we receive for free in

---

34   The verse is Micah 2:13. The ESV translates the Hebrew as "He who opens the breach goes up before them." In German translations, Luther preferred the more martial *Durchbrechen*, "breakthrough." Think of someone smashing through an enemy's line of attack. That one breaking through, disrupting, is Jesus Christ.

Jesus Christ. We humans don't like disruption or interruptions—the lives we prefer are smooth, *hakuna matata*, problem-free. We pine after predictability; we construct orderly storybook appearances. When Jesus Christ stirs things up, disrupts our lives, muddies our comfortable waters, and disturbs our tidy categories, embrace the interruption as part of God's plan for your salvation.

The five-syllable word *transfiguration* is a fancy, theological way of saying a one-syllable word: *change*. Like the action figures called Transformers, Jesus is changed into more than meets the eye.

Never before (and never since) had any human ever seen anything quite like what the inner circle—Peter, James, and John—saw. No Hollywood production with laser lights and digital audio technology could come close to producing the multimedia special effects we see and hear in the transfiguration account (Matthew 17:1–9): the face of Jesus shining, His clothing gloriously glowing with phosphorescent brightness. Lights, camera, action! This was no hologram—Moses showed up, representing the Law of God, and Elijah appeared, representing the Prophets of God. But that was nothing compared to the ultimate showstopper: "a bright cloud overshadowed them, and a voice from the cloud said, 'This is My beloved Son, with whom I am well pleased; listen to Him'" (v. 5).

Even the most distractible person could not help but be riveted to these pyrotechnics. This was a sight for sin-sore eyes; this was God's good news for ears weary with hearing nothing but bad news! We all need this transfiguration, don't we? We all need change! Beloved child, with whom God is well pleased, listen to this word from Romans 12:2: "Do not be conformed to this world, but be *transformed*" (emphasis added). If you peel back the English word *transformed* and dig into the Greek beneath, the Greek word derives from the same root word as the Greek for *transfiguration*. So, not only is Jesus transfigured, but we can hear the Word of God calling us to be transfigured as well, calling each of us to be transformed, calling all of us to be *metamorphized*—which is the Greek word at work here. And how are we changed? "By the renewing of our minds." Our world is starved for real truth, real power, real change. That change—from social change to political change—begins with the work that is worked in us by the One who finally changes death to life, strife to stability, and vanity to righteousness.

Overcoming Disfigurement

In the face of everything that defaces us and degrades us and defiles our God-given dignity, God's promise is fixed, firm, and faithful. We all agree that things need to change in our world—where we disagree is how! In February 2020, Monique and I were visiting with some college students from south Florida. We were presenting at Palm Beach Atlantic University, located in one of the wealthiest communities in the world, and some of the students were complaining that our economic system in the USA is rigged—the rich get richer and the poor get poorer, and we must completely tear down our economic system and start over again to make things right. This visit led me to consider the following and even post about it on social media. Real life is not inhabited without complexity. It comes with unjust rawness as well as inexplicable transcendence. Perhaps that makes for a faulty analogy in comparing it to a game, but without much doubt, the playing field of life is tilted. The rules, moreover, are often unfair, shifting, and tricky. "Winning" always comes from a combination of talent, timing, grit, and luck.

So, while knowing that it's never either/or, which do you and your team primarily prefer overall?

1. To work from the inside, collaborating, but with the goal of gradually improving the rules of the game for yourself and future participants

2. To work from the outside, since collaborators get co-opted, maybe even turning over the game table because the current structure cannot be fixed and needs a revolution

3. To leave the limitations mostly unchallenged, "it won't ever change," equipping ourselves and our youth with the tools to outperform others as effectively and self-protectively as possible

4. Another option

I posed this question on Facebook. Here (with slight modifications for style) is a sampling of the responses:

- **Adam from Atlanta:** As far as I am concerned, trying #1 is ideal, but after ramming your head into walls again and again, #2 looks more and more appealing. I have a great mistrust of institutions and authority though, so that might just be me. When the game is rigged, is there sin in turning over the tables?

- **Todd from St. Catharines, Ontario:** In my 20+ years of experience with parish ministry in the Lutheran Church—Canada, I've gone from #1 (learning that being an immigrant to Canada meant me being ever an "outsider") to #2 and now wholeheartedly #3. I have found outsiders rarely make it into the organism unless there's a major shift in power.

- **Greg from Austin:** The destination determines the path. At one time or another, the players of the game and our relationship with each player have us employing one choice or the other. I prefer #1 as the model for building relationships with participants to effect change. But when called upon, options 2, 3, and 4 are also employed depending on the players of the game.

Some say we need an economic revolution. I disagree! I say we need a spiritual transfiguration with social impact and economic implications. And this starts with *us*! First Peter 4:17 puts it like this: "When it is time for judgment, that judgment begins at the household of God" (my translation). It constitutes an ambitious enough goal to disciple, discipline, and direct the community of faith, never mind expecting to sacralize a secular society. "This is why the church can 'Christianize' politicians and economists but not politics and economics. These 'orders' are ordained by God to remain secular, enjoying a relative (never absolute) autonomy of their own under the sovereign law of the Creator."[35]

Perhaps it would help to compare two concepts: being transfigured (a positive thing) and being disfigured (a negative thing). Being disfigured

---

35 William H. Lazareth, introduction to "The Christian in Society," *LW* 44:xvi.

is the opposite of being transfigured. Being transfigured is what God does to us, blessing us daily; being disfigured is what the devil does to us daily—the stressors, pressures, problems, and distresses of life that wear us down and tear up families and contribute to disease and finally kill us. The disfiguring wage of sin is death.

Being spiritually disfigured is what racism and abuse do to us, especially if we don't deal with our wounds, if our spiritual injuries are not healed; then the person God made us to be slowly gets deformed and distorted. As my friend Reed Lessing puts it, "Unresolved, unmourned grief causes a boatload of problems! So many are stuck in all kinds of bad behavior because they never grieved over an alcoholic dad or an unloving mother or mistreatment or prejudice or bigotry. Rather than actually feeling it, actually grieving over it, actually going through the season of mourning, it's so easy to just put our head down and ignore it."[36]

The healthier, even holier, approach to the messed-up histories that we all carry through life is to own them, face them, embrace them, grace them with forgiveness, learn from them, wash them in the blood-bought promises of Jesus, cast them on His cross, get over them, and get on with life. Life cannot be lived only on the mountaintop or only on Easy Street or only on Happiness Avenue. Peter wanted to stay on the mountaintop, but Jesus leads them back down to the valley, down to a place of betrayal and crucifixion. God sometimes leads us to those places as well. In life, we will suffer. Sorry. Lutherans will tell the truth on this topic. Other religions will promise health, wealth, happiness, and prosperity.

In this life, we will endure long, purple valleys of Lent, but the way to transfiguration is *through* the valley of the shadow of death, and through this valley, there are no shortcuts. But let this sink in: because of your suffering, maybe someone will be saved. This is why we need Jesus and why we need one another; otherwise, the effects of disfigurement can be more than we can bear. That humans are spiritually disfigured shows up in the violence and betrayal and backstabbing we see too often in our communities, such as the February 2020 murder of twenty-year-old Bashar Barakah Jackson, known professionally as Pop Smoke, the Brooklyn rapper who authorities suspect was gunned

---

36   Reed Lessing, *The Book of Job: Blessed Be the Name of the Lord!* Sermon Series (St. Louis: Concordia Seminary Press, 2016).

down by jealous rivals. He frequently boasted about being armed, being dangerous in self-defense, and carrying guns to school and even to church. He was right—no place is safe in a disfigured world. You cannot trust anybody fully, not even yourself. But you can trust Jesus. When the disciples, overwhelmed by the mountaintop apparition, "lifted up their eyes, they saw no one but Jesus only" (Matthew 17:8). And this Jesus died to seal a great deal for you.

Exchanging More

Let's think more about that great deal Jesus made for us. Martin Luther calls what Jesus gives us *der fröhliche Wechsel*, which we might translate today as God's "transfigurational trade deal" for us.[37] In other words, no *change* happens in life without a spiritual *exchange*: God gives to us the blessings we don't deserve in exchange for the sin He takes away. Jesus Christ is not only the Lamb of God who takes away the sin of the world, who takes away what disfigures us. But He also gives us something great in exchange for the sin He takes away; He gives us something that transfigures us.

Neither we nor any other individual can fit neatly into preformed boxes. None of us is just one or even two things, nor even the same things two days in a row. The narrow boxes of identity that pigeonholers dump others into are far too thin for human habitation. And I'd say that goes double for people who realize that they—like every person born of woman—are created in the image of an infinite God who is to be worshiped as Father, Son, and Spirit.

For example, I am a Jamaican-born, Canadian-raised US citizen residing on the outskirts of New York City. I was reborn through Baptism in a Methodist church in Montego Bay. I am also a citizen of God's kingdom without any denomination—my ultimate home. I am a child of a loving heavenly Father with an African-descended human father and a Scotch-Irish mother. My surname, Nunes, carries mysterious roots—Sephardic Jewish. My Savior is Mary's son and God's Son,

---

37   For more on this, see Alberto García and John Nunes, "God of Justification, God of Life: A Borderland Reimagining of the Reformation," in *Wittenberg Meets the World: Reimagining the Reformation at the Margins* (Grand Rapids: Eerdmans, 2017), 25–26.

a Palestinian named Jesus, who's called the Christ. I am called to be a husband to Monique, a father to six grown children, and a grandfather to an expanding entourage of eleven so far. Secondarily, I am called by the Spirit to be a pastor within the evangelical-catholic (Lutheran) tradition, a president of a Christian college, and a professor of English, ethics, and theology. I have one degree from a higher educational institution affiliated with The Lutheran Church—Missouri Synod (the group that comprises my earthly spiritual home), one from an institution of the Lutheran Church—Canada, and two from an institution of the Evangelical Lutheran Church in America. I am a saint and a sinner, defined by time and space, limited by resources and abilities, but forgiven by the unlimited God I strive to serve.

I am not alone in my complex identity that resists categorization—which is why we all need less of *they* and *them* and more of *us*. Less of categories and more of taking people for who they are, for who God made them to be, just people for whom Jesus died, for whom He was transfigured so that we could experience transfiguration. As we receive God's healing grace and as we receive people healingly as they are, we can become bridge builders who break boundaries and broker hope.

"And we all, with unveiled face, beholding the glory of the Lord, are being transformed into the same image from one degree of glory to another. For this comes from the Lord who is the Spirit" (2 Corinthians 3:18). This Spirit is *the* change agent who will turn

- **persecution into possibilities,**

- **oppression into opportunities,**

- **divisive mutations into diverse mutuality,**

- **messes into miracles,**

- **burdens into blessings,**

- **trials into triumphs,**

- **tests into testimonies,**

- **selfish individualism into interdependent personhood, and**

- **enemies into allies.**

9

THANKING MORE

*W*alking through a convention gathering in Minneapolis, I exchanged casual greetings with a woman I was passing by. "And how are you doing?" I inquired in reply to her greeting.

At first, I thought she was saying something rather customary, "Great!" But in milliseconds her response finished with "Grate . . . ful!"

I stopped and turned on a dime back toward her. "What possessed you to say that?" I inquired.

"Well, the more you say it," she replied, "the more you see it."

The more we thank God for all the good gifts we have received, the more we will see the Giver at work in all people, places, and things; thus, rather than grousing so quickly about what grates us, by the Spirit, we can grow in being grateful, learning to "give thanks in all circumstances; for this is the will of God in Christ Jesus for you" (1 Thessalonians 5:18).

There is no shortage of evidence of what Martin Luther called "the abominable sin of ingratitude and forgetfulness of [God's] blessings."[38] I overheard some of that ingratitude and forgetfulness one day in the gate area of LaGuardia Airport from "that guy," a gentleman on his phone in broadcast mode. With astringent tones, he was griping as if we couldn't hear him, as if we were not there, as if his sense of entitlement had deafened him to the volume of his own voice. Captive to his

---

38 *LW* 46:258.

decibels, we all learned that his life had become, as he summarized, "basically unlivable." Apparently, his parents were traveling in Bali, and his apartment was under renovation, so he was forced to stay in a two-bedroom loft in Tribeca. "I'm basically homeless! I need my therapist!" Sir, at this moment—I devotionally said to myself—I'm praying that you see your therapist soon and that she or he opens your eyes and closes your mouth.

Or perhaps your ears need to feed your heart with a liberating word of Law to prepare you to hear, heed, and speak Good News: "These are grumblers, malcontents, following their own sinful desires; they are loud-mouthed boasters, showing favoritism to gain advantage" (Jude 16). Regardless, poverty is multidimensional, and not all of it has to do with material assets; some has to do with deficits of gratitude. From such, in others and in ourselves, deliver us, good Lord. Just because we're well-to-do doesn't mean we're not meant for more; in fact, the higher up we go, the closer to the front of the expectation line we might find ourselves, or as Jesus puts it: "From everyone who has been given much, much will be demanded" (Luke 12:48 NIV).

Given More

Doing well economically and doing good socially must go together. "In all things I have shown you that by working hard in this way we must help the weak and remember the words of the Lord Jesus, how He Himself said, 'It is more blessed to give than to receive'" (Acts 20:35). Yes, work more, make more money, gain more good privilege and usable power so that you can do more, help more, influence more, and give more.

The president and CEO of a global, Fortune 500 hotel chain was scheduled to speak for commencement one year at Valparaiso University. At the last minute, we learned that his hotel reservations had not yet been confirmed.

I called up the local property in the chain of which he is the president: "Hello, I'm calling to inquire about rooms."

The woman answering the phone replied, "Um, sir, do you happen to know that it's commencement weekend? All of our rooms have been booked for months!"

Courteously, I added, "What a coincidence. It's your CEO who's speaking at our event who needs this room."

To which she quickly quipped, "Yeah, right."

"No, I'm serious. Check our school's website; you'll see him."

The desk lady left the phone for one minute and returned with the announcement, "We just so happen to have one room remaining for your guest—a suite!"

But this corporate leader has used his wealth, his privilege, his advantage to contribute time, money, and wisdom both to his local Lutheran congregation and to international causes such as ending malaria. So-called "privilege" represents a stewardship opportunity, a chance to use one's resources and resourcefulness in order to promote social entrepreneurism and provide access to those without it. Consider this definition of *privilege*: it relates to the special power, opportunity, or immunity granted to some individuals or groups as contrasted with other individuals or groups. It refers to a position in society. There is little one can do about such status or its conferral. It comes about because of how humans are wired. It's either inherited or earned or given by God or purchased or stolen or you're born with it or some combination of the above. What you *can* do something about is your *disposition* toward others based on your *position* in society. That question is undergirded by one's theological perspective.

Goodbye, Diamond

While I was president and CEO of Lutheran World Relief, my position required significant travel. We worked beyond the end of the road, but it took Delta Airlines and its global partners to courier me to the beginning of the end of the road. My life is now rooted in the USA, requiring far fewer miles of airplane travel. Adios, Diamond Status. At this point in my life, for the sake of my health, my family, and for me, that's just fine—except that it means a reduction in what they call "status," resulting in fewer upgrades to first-class seating. As I took my leave from a life of free wine and extra wide seats, here are a few lessons from years of flying amidst the "elite."

1. Privilege is definitely addictive. Being spoiled does not engender gratitude; rather, it breeds an expectation for more spoiling.

2. Passenger behavior, especially common courtesy toward flight attendants and fellow passengers, does not improve with more privileges. Drama does, however. The most elite travelers sometimes have the most self-entitled, entertainingly pubescent public tantrums.

3. Mothers traveling alone with small children—I can count the dads with kids I've seen on one hand—should automatically be upgraded to first class. They've got their hands full already and could benefit from some extra attention and perks.

4. The meals are the most overrated features of first class—too much salt, MSG, and microwaving.

5. Though chattier, the less pampered passengers in economy class are friendlier, slimmer, and soberer. At least that's how I'm consoling myself for my new life in sardine-can seating.

Nothing gets in the way of justice more efficiently than self-centeredness. Justice that misses the point that some have been given by God more than others for a reason, justice that's for "just us"—that's the essence of sin, to be turned in on oneself or on one's own group only. I like to say that the middle letter in the following words is a gigantic *I*: sIn, prIde, trIbe. The work of empathy, which is necessary for human survival, is much more difficult when you can't see past that *I*.

Recently, I was snarled in a traffic jam of shopping carts at a chaotic warehouse store, and I was disappointed with my reaction. While it was short-lived, I had some negativity toward some of the "outsiders" and newcomers to the USA filling the aisles. Three musings—as Monique got good deals—helped to cure my momentary bad attitude: (1) John, how dare you act like an entitled "insider" when you once carried a green card? (2) John, have you noticed the medical and military uniforms worn by some of these immigrants and so-called minorities? Those you deem "outsiders" are protecting you and now compose an emerging majority of those providing you with healthcare. You need them! (3) John, do you not reside in a nation that is dynamic precisely because of those who add their accents to our sound, their spices to our shelves, and their different sense of personal space to our crowds, even while spending their hard-earned dollars in our disheveled big-box stores?

In such a pluralistic society, it is naturally more difficult to be empathetic; but when motivated by God's love toward everyone, such empathy is like an emotional HVAC system. It moderates the temperature of a social environment and sets up an atmospheric control where conversations of mutual respect and relationships of mutual responsibility can flourish. We all need something from someone. We all owe something to someone.

The promises of God and the benefits of Christ are applied savingly to the lives of everyone who trusts the work of the Spirit through Word and Sacraments—what the Lutheran Confessions refer to as the "media of the Spirit." I do love that phrase as pointing to the Word, Absolution, Baptism, Eucharist, and the fellowship—indicative of the way the Spirit works grace and strengthens faith in the lives of believers. It seems to me that this is God's preferred (and most dependable to hang on to) way of working, inasmuch as God loves these media. Matter does, in fact, matter. And this life of salvation is meant for more than believers to enjoy and keep to themselves—it's meant for their families, their villages, their communities, for the world. God is a God of justice, but justice for *just us* is not what the loving Father had in mind. We are, simply, meant for more.

More Privilege

Two truths I've learned from my students, most of whom are the strivers that I, an immigrant, also once was: First, sometimes it's not a lack of courage, virtue, or hard work (despite what some might say) that leads to failure; rather, it's a lack of opportunity, resources, or connections. And second, it's not because I lack vision or dreams for the future (despite what some others might say) that I speak mostly in the past tense, the historical, from memory; it's that I'm what they're not—old. My hard-earned wisdom tells me that much of what passes as outward success isn't as much earned as it is a result of privilege, a gift. What exudes here is the sense of what most of us carry through our lives: we are all meant for more, but without certain privilege, we remain with a song in our soul that never gets sung, a dream for heroic achievement that never gets done.

So, any position, any privilege, any righteousness we have is a gift that gives us traction for action in this world. That's the Christian perspective. To forget this leads to self-righteousness. Self-righteousness and privilege feed off of each other. A disposition of self-righteousness tends to lead people to see themselves as privileged, and those who are privileged tend to be vulnerable to becoming self-righteous. Their disposition toward others cannot but be callous, self-centered, and self-absorbed. They aren't bothered by saying yes to themselves and no to others. Curtained behind their pride, they cannot see past their entitlement to the dignity that all people inherently possess. I pity such people—and myself when I am that person—because we are all meant for more. Those whose go-to is to ridicule others or consider themselves inherently superior to others just because they possess certain privileges are living below what God intended. They can't see how they are meant for more than treating others as stepping-stones to their destination. They can't see how ugly they have become. They cannot see because either their consciences have become dulled to hearing the voice of their Maker or they have never developed such a spiritual sensitivity.

Not so with the authentically righteous. They have heard and answered the call of the Holy Spirit. They see their position in society as an opportunity. Saying no to oneself becomes possible when your life is captive to the yes from Jesus. Faith in His Good News produces a life-altering humility—it's part of your refurbished disposition. Those set free by the Spirit are heartbroken when they cannot find ways to extend God's yes to other humans, to provide access to privilege, especially for strivers and survivors. Blessed are those with a disposition to hear the groans of creation, to respond to the hopes of others, to exuberate with attitudes of gratitude, irrespective of their position in life.

10

RAGING MORE

ven if you only occasionally glance at the TV, you may have seen them. Those posters that sneak into the camera shot at sporting events, emblazoned with an ironically cryptic Bible verse, just two numbers separated by a colon and preceded by a personal name: "John 3:16." Next to this, the most noteworthy Bible verse du jour might be Micah 6:8. The call to "do justice, and to love kindness, and to walk humbly"—the "with your God" part, modifying the manner of "walking," is sometimes included and sometimes omitted—is paraded as a proof-text for much so-called politically correct public discourse of our time. Because of its growing frequency and familiarity, the historical and textual context, not to mention the primary meaning of this text, can be lost in these pop culture displays. More critically, the domesticating popularity of "Micah 6:8" tends to overlook the urgency of a fiery, angry God who—according to the same prophet—melts mountains and splits open valleys (1:4).

Micah 6:8 is a key verse for Christians involved in ministries of compassion. Many younger adults find social service as a key to putting their faith into action. They are attracted to connecting the Sunday Divine Service with being in service to the world, ending global poverty, addressing injustice, fighting for the rights of the unborn, ameliorating human suffering. In the face of these challenges, prophetic preachers within the evangelical-catholic tradition of our own time must, at times, take on a righteous rage as they consider the unintelligible evils of our world. As they do, however, they may reflect on the wisdom of habituating their angry tones within at least two considerations, drawn from the Old Testament prophets.

First, ancient preachers did not fume for the sake of evildoers' death but rather for their life (Ezekiel 18:32). In our contemporary preaching, as in our religion, the Gospel predominates, always for the sake of the life of the world—even when dealing with harsh prophetic texts.

Second, the prophets did not fume apart from also entering incarnationally into the pain of the people. In the paradoxical pattern of incarnational ministry, their affliction is both/and: not only over against the "wickedness in the house of the wicked" (Micah 6:10) but also alongside and with the affliction of sin (Isaiah 63:9).

The opening scene of Micah reveals a divine charge, a "witness" (1:2) against a treacherous people who have made a mess of God's promise. Though led by God miraculously across dry land into liberation (6:4), they have now crossed God. "The best of them is like a brier" (7:4). Micah calls out the people for their specific moral breakdown, whether personal crookedness or public corruption.

The just anger of God at this particular human injustice filled Micah and spilled over into his preaching: "Woe to those who devise wickedness and work evil on their beds! When the morning dawns, they perform it, because it is in the power of their hand. They covet fields and seize them, and houses, and take them away; they oppress a man and his house, a man and his inheritance" (2:1–2).

What a mellifluous message it must have been in the ears of ordinary farmers. When the Messiah comes, these who are terrorized by people who confiscate their property "shall dwell secure" (5:4)! What a joyous delight in the hearts of those who had suffered violent removal from their places of livelihood to hear of a judge who would bring peace, under whom they could "beat . . . swords into plowshares" and turn "spears into pruning hooks" (4:3).

The modern-day versions of these subsistence farmers continue to suffer egregiously. They are the one-quarter of the world's population that produces just enough food, fiber, fuel, or raw materials to support and feed their immediate families. Their dependence on the land makes them vulnerable to the capricious covetousness of those who would illegally, unethically, and sinfully seize their property. *Parrhesia* is a

Spirit-fired, brutal candor to plunge with confessional courage into the face of threat and challenge from regnant structures.

Who will speak out on behalf of those whose voices are unheard? Everyone has a voice; no one is voiceless. But some voices are ignored, squelched, or silenced. In order to advocate more for those who are oppressed, sometimes it takes anger to draw attention to injustice.

More Justice-Doing

Justice relates to judgments that do something about what is fair and right. Justice is a transcendent ideal that cannot be contained in any single sociological category or political domain. But justice is more than an arbiter of right and wrong. Justice is something that we must act on, treating people according to our belief that every single human person possesses inherent dignity, value, and worth and that every life has meaning and purpose. From conception to natural death, all individuals are possessors of a higher inheritance, irrespective of their academic degree or social pedigree.

When we think about doing more works of love in this world, let these words from Martin Luther echo in our ears: The Word of God always comes first. "After it follows faith; after faith, love; then love does every good work, for . . . it is the fulfilling of the law."[39] It doesn't start with the work itself, it originates from God's Word. Apart from God's grace, made known in the Word and Sacraments, "we remain crooked men walking crooked miles and end up being hell to one another in a crooked house."[40] But with God's grace, the disparate, previously divergent dichotomies of our lives being to align, start to straighten, to integrate for the sake of integrity.

How we believe, how we live, and how we pray all go together. Or for you Latin lovers, *lex credendi, lex orandi, lex vivendi*. *Lex credendi* means the rule of faith (what we believe), which both informs and is informed by *lex orandi*, the rule of prayer (how we pray and praise),

---

39 *LW* 36:39.

40 Martin Franzmann, "Who Is a God Like Thee?" *The Springfielder* 38, no. 2 (September 1973): 81–83.

which both informs and is informed by *lex vivendi*, the rule of living (leading honorable and just lives).

Fighting More! For What?

Compared to some tragedies of tribalism, the following example might seem trite, but it illustrates the silly spirals that can arise when local, tribal truths seek to supplant God's transcendent truth. The only component of this story I've changed are the names and places—to protect the guilty. Pastor Avery Webster was assigned to his vicarage (an internship for pastors) in 1980 at Schmidts' Lutheran Church in Hercules, South Carolina. "I was also told at the time that there were three Lutheran churches on the same intersection, but in all honesty, it didn't mean a whole lot to me until I arrived there and learned the history." As legend has it, three families came over from Germany in the early 1800s: the Hausers, the Buchheimers, and the Schmidts. Early on, the Schmidts said, "We will donate land for a church if you name it after us!" And it was agreed upon. Schmidts' Lutheran Church.

Some years later, the Hausers and Buchheimers got mad at the Schmidts because they began to think they actually owned Schmidts' Lutheran Church, so the other two families split off to form their own church directly across the street and called it St. Paul's Lutheran Church. Some years later, the Buchheimers got mad at the Hausers and split again, bought land on the same corner across the street, and were not going to let the *other* St. Paul's take their name, so they called it St. Paul's as well. It became a bit confusing over the years with two St. Paul's Lutheran churches on the same corner, so the Buchheimer church, since it was located at a slightly higher elevation, quickly became known at St. Paul's Upper, to which it is still referred to this day.

It gets worse. There is a cemetery on the fourth corner, with graves of all three families buried there. The Buchheimers wanted the cemetery for themselves, mainly for the funerals of the Buchheimers, but the Hausers would not offer it to them. So, they took it to court and of course, the court would have nothing to do with it. What do you do when you can't acquire a cemetery? You sneak in during the middle of the night (as the Buchheimers did) and build a brick foundation wall around all the Buchheimer plots so you will not have to lay beside the dead bodies of the Hausers until Christ comes again!

"It has been quite a few years since I have been there," Pastor Webster reports, "but the last time I visited, there was still tension on the corner."

This true story is an insightful example of what happens when tribalism goes bad! I wonder what sorts of tribalism we possess that others will find trivial, silly, stupid, and sad one hundred years from now. We must remember that we humans are complex creatures; this does not change because of redemption. Jesus sums up human anthropology with this analogy: "If you then, who are evil, know how to give good gifts to your children, how much more will your Father who is in heaven give good things to those who ask Him!" (Matthew 7:11).

I wonder what we say to God when we pray for our enemies. Do we consider beginning the prayer in humility, with the recognition that we ourselves might be the problem, with confession? There are basically two ways: (1) Ask God to give them justice with the rage of an imprecatory psalmist. "Blessed shall he be who takes your little ones and dashes them against the rock!" (Psalm 137:9). Or this way: (2) Ask God to show them the same mercy He demonstrated to you and then leave them in God's hands, with the assurance that at the end of the day, when "your life is hid with Christ in God" (Colossians 3:3 KJV), those who are coming at you or coming for you would be wise to think twice about crossing paths with the Keeper of your hideout.

More Positivity

But how do we maintain a positive, Christ-centered approach in the midst of enemies? Is positivity even possible anymore in our culture of digital instantaneity and multimedia spontaneity? Even while an event or a conversation is yet ongoing, people rush to judgment, and the truth gets trampled. No one wants to appear naive, so negativity becomes the go-to. Of course, cynicism isn't new among young people; it's almost innate. In a good sense, the doubts of youth serve to wake us up and make us more aware of our hypocrisies. However, what I'm finding difficult in this environment is keeping college students confident about our American experiment. Many of them are deeply suspicious that our elected leaders seem to care most about power, self-preservation, and politics, or politricks.

It's not so much about which side did what to the other; it's that with as many gargantuan problems that the US government should be working together to address, we too often are distracted by what feels to young people to be more about partisan posturing and power plays than about principle. It's difficult to disagree with their skepticism; it's easy to point blame back and forth across the aisle rather than to expect better behavior from the whole kit and caboodle. We must pray and work for more mutual respect, rationality, and accountability among our highest officeholders.

People of faith, those held by the Spirit in the thrall of the One who is the summit and source of all that is good, we have opportunity here to appeal to the better natures, the higher selves of those with whom we are in relationship. Such an elevated path, already difficult to find, feels decreasingly available in these hyper-reactionary, smugly cynical, instantaneous times. It's easier, safer, and looks sophisticated to be a dispassionate, detached, nonchalant, insouciantly cool observer of the world's circus—behaving like you are above and beyond involvement with the ordinary clowns. Moreover, no one debates whether or not there's an overabundance of trouble in life. Human sinfulness and our corresponding structures of sin have ensured the presence of problems in perpetuity on earth. The Holy Spirit is fully aware of this temptation to become cynical, overwhelmed, or worn out. This is why He urges us: "And let us not grow weary of doing good, for in due season we will reap, if we do not give up" (Galatians 6:9).

Road-Rage Interactions

Like gawkers slowing to gape at a crash scene, our cultural mood seems perversely attracted to road-rage interactions, whether in traffic, on the internet, on reality TV, or in plain old real life. Fights draw fascinated onlookers. A Christian discipline—try it in Advent or Lent—might be to promote thoughtfulness in the sense of looking away and not rushing to judgment; not blasting away first, but actually asking questions and seeking facts; engaging others with respect and decisiveness—treating others with dignity ought not to be equated with being wishy-washy; and putting the best construction on the motivations of others (see the Eighth Commandment) as they, like all of us, struggle to navigate their way through this bizarre journey called life.

We too often forget a truth about this world. Though it is breathtakingly beautiful, it is also devastatingly broken; though, as the poet Gerard Manley Hopkins puts it, it is "charged with the grandeur of God," it is also flawed by the utter foolishness of humans. In such a world, why would we even for a split second expect people to put the best construction on our words, actions, or motivations on, say, Facebook, when you and I struggle to keep this command toward others at, say, church? Only a hypocrite should act shocked!

Before scoffing at how evil this world is, consider this. We are the ones who know more about how low Jesus had to go to take up the cross of forgiveness (which was for everyone, not only for Christians), and therefore we should be rising from our own gutters of gossip. Before scolding others, we who know we've been claimed by Father, Son, and Spirit must lay hold of the very virtues we claim to hold; the ethical systems we place on others flow, in the first place, from faith!

I believe that Western understandings of morality and justice were built primarily—for better or worse—by the Western Christian tradition. But this project is incomplete and messy, in part because the church has its own architecture to shore up, its own house to get in order, and will for as long as the earth lasts. But being imperfect does not disqualify us from raising our prophetic voices, calling for a higher standard. We must never forget we are both fully forgiven and fully works-in-progress. So, without scoffing or scolding, we keep working because the church knows better than any other entity that we are *all* meant for more, far more.

11

NEIGHBORING MORE

hristians specialize in talking about loving our neighbors. This makes sense since they know that there is no sense of being a responsible Christian citizen that is isolated from being responsive to others in their need. We are particularly articulate in our concern for faraway neighbors in places such as Haiti, Tajikistan, or other economically impoverished nations. The word *neighbor*, however, derives from "near dweller." The problem is that we tend to think about our neighbor in meaningless abstractions and miss the particular, the flesh-and-blood reality, the actual person suffering and asking for help. Your neighbor may have an address or be homeless, may be undocumented or unemployed, but nevertheless remains a near-dweller. *Neighbor*, for Christians, is a real and present word, not a hypothetical or abstract phenomenon.

I was blessed to participate in the investiture of Yolanda Tanner on November 10, 2010, when she was sworn in as a judge for the Eighth Circuit Court for Baltimore City. I shared this prayer:

> We thank You, O God of all, for the joy of this day, for the radiant sunshine, for the divine favor You have invested in each of us. Help us to uphold, with respect, all who occupy seats of responsibility and authority: judges, juries, lawyers, and law officers.
>
> Guard our judicial system from corruption and prejudice so that, with fairness, rights are protected and freedoms are preserved.

> Rouse us all into an increasing awareness of the everyday ways in which every one of us is called to serve the global human family.
>
> This day, gracious God, we pray especially for Your child Yolanda, that You would continue to pour out Your Spirit upon her—the Spirit of wisdom and understanding, the Spirit of impartiality and the good use of power, the Spirit of knowledge and the fear of the Lord. In Your name, we ask and expect every blessing. I pray in Jesus. Amen.

I was blessed to participate in this event, and in North America and most of the Western world, we are all blessed with democratic freedoms, with opportunities to live out our faith for neighbors who need to see it and feel it.

We can often neglect those opportunities though, and I consider that neglect idiotic. *Idiot* is a word used by the ancient Greeks to describe a nonparticipant in the public square and its political processes. It's literally derived from their pronoun for oneself, as in sticking to oneself—though it might incidentally also describe those who abdicate their responsibilities, surrender their rights, and vacate their roles as citizens of our liberal democracy. Read. Speak out. Register. Vote. Pray in public. Be responsible.

When I use the word *idiot*, I don't mean to ridicule others. That would be irresponsible. It's a healthy sign of humility to laugh at oneself, and the Scriptures attest to this: "A joyful heart is good medicine" (Proverbs 17:22). But there's something a bit sick about one who takes pleasure in enervating others; the same proverb continues "a crushed spirit dries up the bones." If your presence doesn't give health to your neighbors but instead crushes them, ridicules them, you might want to reconsider your strategy to better align it with the divine design.

Being responsible does not mean burying one's head in the sand of a risk-free personal morality, nor shaking one's head publicly at some sinner exposed, nor burrowing oneself in a heady, philosophically sound ethical code. Responsibility must include being responsive to others. Choosing to ignore the cries of children in a burning building, taking no relevant action, "what a shame that they should burn!"—such nonresponses would never be considered responsible. See something and say something, dream something and do something, preach something and practice something. Every community has someone silently shrieking in fear: how can I be a hearer and a healer under the influence of the Spirit by whom we are called to be responsible? We all make mistakes. The dock is a safe position in the harbor, but ships are meant to be sailed, even out into waters as choppy as these times in which we find ourselves.

Vulture Culture

We are entering a time I call vulture culture. Some place themselves above their neighbors, feeding on the latest buzz. Others crave, like buzzards, the carcasses of negative news, half-dead carnivores gobbling up the dead meat of gossip. Then there are the intellectual elites who like to think their thinking and theorizing sets them above—but they are sometimes positioned so far "above" that they are detached from the place where the rubber of life hits the road of reality. The best positioning to make a lasting difference is in, with, and under. The lives of the wise are as invested as they are interested in tackling tough topics with redemptive conversations that revert to high ideals and virtuous ideas. I'm not certain this comes naturally to anyone, but we have opportunities in our ordinary lives to develop habits through everyday acts of extraordinary love.

Ships are meant to be sailed, even out into waters as choppy as these times in which we find ourselves.

Standing *over* others—rather than accompanying them, standing *with* them—and treating others as if we matter more than they would be the opposite of Paul's counterintuitive wisdom, which cuts across class, culture, and caste: "In humility count others more significant than yourselves" (Philippians 2:3).

When I worked for Lutheran World Relief, headquartered in downtown Baltimore, every day that I walked to work I'd pass by a woman who lived a crushed existence on the street, among cardboard boxes and tattered bags filled with odds and ends. This woman, whose name nobody knew, was a talker: "You're really just like me," she shouted out one day. "One step away from death, and there but by the grace of God you could be in my shoes."

The daily damnations she experienced by having no fixed address prepared her to be an outdoor preacher; as Martin Luther once wrote, "Living, indeed, dying and being damned make a theologian," not seminary education or academic achievement.[41] I must admit that more than once I tried to avoid her, but there was no way to avert her penetrating eyes or ignore her piercing insights. With a crackling, staccato voice, she spun clever truisms about the universality of trouble and troublemakers. Through blue sighs of lyrical despair, she articulated what so many of us know to be true but in our plastic pride can't bear to admit. One of her classic phrases I'll never forget: "God don't like ugly and He ain't too impressed with pretty."

The Spirit of God often has a way of confronting us through ordinary people—even those we consider subordinary. We get faced with God truths that may not only annoy us but also strip away our laminated camouflages, expose our egocentric sins, devastate our defenses; then we, led forth defenseless, can be repurposed, that is, given a new purpose for life in Christ. This nameless street saint took every opportunity to be such a difference-maker. If she with nothing could do it, then surely we with much can at least strive to do so too.

---

41 Translated from Martin Luther, *D. Martin Luthers Werke: Kritische Gesamtausgabe* (Weimar: Hermann Böhlau, 1892), 5:163.

Daring More

In the 1970s, reggae superstar Bob Marley recorded a song addressing social injustice titled "So Much Trouble in the World." Marley, who received a Christian Baptism in the Ethiopian Orthodox Church in the last year of his life, brought attention to many problems afflicting the masses of Jamaicans living in poverty. He saw himself as a prophetic inhabitant of a planet plagued with racial oppression, moral confusion, global unrest, and economic corruption—so much trouble in the world.

BOB MARLEY

Marley was echoing unknowingly the indictment of Martin Luther in his explanation of the prayer "Give us our daily bread": "How much trouble there is now in the world only on account of . . . daily oppression . . . [and] raising of prices . . . by those who greedily oppress the poor."[42]

Ordinary Christian citizens—in the ordinary places we live, love, work, play, and pray—can construct pathways out of poverty for others by committing to the principle of access. I'm working with this idea that people living in poverty need access more than anything: access to education, to employment opportunities, to networks of influence, to residential options, to reliable childcare, to dependable transportation, to healthy food options, to quality healthcare, to investment capital, to markets.

Theologically speaking, we should never justify the inevitability of socioeconomic poverty. Yes, Jesus did remark, "The poor you will always have with you" (Matthew 26:11 NIV), but that does not mean we don't work to end human suffering. We will always have disease with us; that doesn't mean we don't run marathons to raise dollars to support research to end breast cancer. We will always have car accidents; that doesn't mean we don't have laws to increase safety by wearing seat belts and not driving while impaired. We will always have sin with us; that doesn't mean we don't preach against it. In fact, according to the Scriptures, the opposite is the case: "There will never cease to be poor in the land. Therefore I command you, 'You shall open wide your hand . . . to the needy and to the poor, in your land'" (Deuteronomy 15:11).

As we support access, be aware of some myths that oversimplify the causes of poverty. One myth places blame on the individual. This first narrative contends that the prime causes of poverty are a lack of know-how or the absence of individual initiative, poor personal discipline, or family breakdown. The second myth is that poverty is primarily caused by systems of injustice and oppression. This second narrative attributes blame not to the individual but to society, within history, because of structures. Neither myth will likely ever be fully dethroned because both possess truths, but a commitment to access can destabilize both.

---

42   LC III 84.

The first myth can be destabilized because a genuine possibility of real access serves as a motivator for humans to develop their capacity, qualifications, and relationships. When people living in poverty can sense that the avenues of access, pathways to possibility, and gateways to opportunity are palpable, they are often then drawn out of their debilitating circumstances. Hope is a colossal motivator. When people previously deprived of it catch a spark of it, progress happens.

Second, as we intentionally contribute our small part by ensuring access—not through legislation or arbitration—but through choosing to use our privileges for the sake of others—we are leveling the playing field for "outsiders," expanding circles of respect, and theologically recognizing the image of God in everybody. This destabilizes the second myth.

When considering our role in expanding access, there are many practical, infrastructural needs that should not be bypassed: for example, people living in poverty often reside in communities that lack support elements to access, like safety and security, sufficient rule of law, a community of encouragement that values education—these are not always available in marginalized communities eking out subsistence-level lives. These variables must be factored in when considering what mitigates against or is additive to access. An oft-repeated aphorism, coined perhaps by economist Glenn Loury, is "One by one, from the inside out." If we each do a little more, with a lot more love, the aggregate benefit will be unspeakable.

On the other hand, when purveyors of charity are self-centered, not recognizing the One who pursues us all with "goodness and mercy," empathy becomes difficult. Despite being well-motivated, such acts of mercy tend to accomplish the opposite of what they intend by contributing to structural injustice; displaying attitudes of arrogance and paternalism, even if unwittingly; and reinforcing relationships of power versus powerlessness or, worse, a ruling class of privileged experts versus an underclass seen as ignoramuses incapable of being anything more than charitable recipients. *We*, if we must divide ourselves, are meant for more and so are *they*.

12

DEMONSTRATING MORE

*F*aith is a living, unshakable confidence in God's grace."[43] We all fall short in daring to demonstrate that unshakable face of grace to those who need it. I have a story of a time this shortage applied to me. Parenting takes energy. Monique and I agree it's the kind of energy suited best for people younger in years than we. And while we don't ordinarily consider ourselves to be old, whatever that means, we are blessed to have eleven grandchildren. Our children enjoy giving us the opportunity to engage in grandparenting. (Once when I typed "grandparenting," it was autocorrected to "grandpa renting." I don't intend on taking this personally when the kids drop off their kids.)

Life zips by with seemingly accelerating quickness. That tempo seems to speed up even faster when we are visited by our grandchildren— especially our hyped-up grandsons, whom we love, when they invade our house with such raw intensity. We are convinced that whatever active ingredient they put in energy drinks is harvested from these boys. For example, on one eventful Saturday afternoon, there came to us three grandsons, all under age 7. The room they occupied and destroyed was called appropriately "the grandkids' room." Monique had labored for months to transform this space into being both child-friendly and beautiful. But the wall hangings were knocked off

---

43 Martin Luther, "Preface to the Letter of St. Paul to the Romans," trans. Brother Andrew Thornton, OSB (St. Anselm Abbey, 1983), https://www.ccel.org/l/luther/romans/pref_romans.html.

and various ornaments came crashing down and the ceiling fan has wobbled dangerously since. In this room, we made the mistake of a putting a bunk bed, which, needless to say, we intended for sleeping.

But by these three masterpieces, these veritable pieces of God's handiwork, that bed was transformed into a two-tiered trampoline, the twin bed on top and a larger queen size below. Over and over again they all went up the ladder, from where they launched the three-year-old from the top—several times grazing, if not hanging from, the ceiling fan. He went repeatedly, squealing with glee, through the air and landed on the crash-pad bed on bottom.

Hearing this uproarious commotion, I immediately made my way with quickness *away* from them downstairs to my study to hide. But I could hear Monique lay down the law from down the hall: "STOP. You are going to hurt yourselves!" Then she texted me, "John, where are you? I need help."

I pretended not to see her text message. It was a mix of believing that a prophet is without honor in his own home, knowing what terror the ancients exacted on the messengers, and fearing for my life. It was calculated. I'd much rather take my chances with falling into the hands of an angry Monique, who is at least capable of showing mercy, than into the hands of my own terrifying offspring.

With no other option to save them from themselves and because she cares compassionately for them, it became necessary for Monique, quite God-like, to go in herself. God's love doesn't run or retreat from trouble. He gets involved—not to critique or analyze or judge (John 3:17), but to save. I viewed

MONIQUE

JOHN, WHERE ARE YOU?
I NEED HELP

them as wretchedly wild, destructive beings; Monique viewed them as masterpieces who were worth risking her life. My wife is more like Jesus than I. But with the Lord there is forgiveness (Psalm 130:4). Daily! As I remember my Baptism, three splashes of grace for me, the face of grace, Jesus Christ, for me!

Daring to demonstrate more means living with more trust, not in the enormity of what you see, nor in the paucity of courage you see within yourself, but in the untried, unfelt, untested, unpredictable, unanticipatable goodness of God. To pour out oneself in such service is to see light that was previously eclipsed by fear. "If you pour yourself out for the hungry and satisfy the desire of the afflicted, then shall your light rise in the darkness and your gloom be as the noonday" (Isaiah 58:10).

More Discontented?

"You have made us for Yourself," St. Augustine pined longingly. Then he pointed to his and our fundamental discontentment: "Our hearts are restless until they rest in You."[44] As long as we are walking on the soil of this third, blue rock from the sun, we will experience that mix of contentment and discontentment. Should we become contented? Yes and no. "Keep your life free from love of money, and be content with what you have, for [God] has said, 'I will never leave you nor forsake you'" (Hebrews 13:5). Be contented with the commitments you have made in life, to a spouse, to a cause, even to a denomination. Be contented with your limits, your limitations, your natural boundaries.

But we should never rest easy with injustices, with any assaults on life from the womb to the tomb. We cannot become contented with mediocrity nor any smallness of love nor coldness of hospitality nor any narrow kindness found within our lives.

---

44   Translated from Augustine, *Confessions* 1:1.

~~~~~~~~~~~~~~~~~~~~~~~~~~~~~

O GIVER OF VIRTUOUS RESTLESSNESS, KEEP US FROM SELF-RIGHTEOUS PUFFERY. AS WE STRIVE FOR JUSTICE, BE OUR JOY. O LIFTER OF WEIGHTY COMPLACENCY, KEEP US FROM LUKEWARM-NESS. AS WE TAKE A PAUSE FROM THE RUTHLESS PACE OF LIFE, BE OUR PEACE. O SIGNATURE OF BAPTISMAL MEANING, TRACE OUR LIVES WITH THE CROSS. KEEP US FROM BEING EITHER COLDHEARTED OR HOTHEADED. AS WE FACE THE DIABOLICAL ENTANGLEMENTS THROWN ACROSS OUR PATHS, BE OUR FREEDOM IN JESUS. AMEN.

~~~~~~~~~~~~~~~~~~~~~~~~~~~~~

Graduation celebrations are the payoff day in academic circles. They are the receipt for hard work not only by students who celebrate but also by faculty and staff who joy in getting students to the finishing line. Graduates, indeed, should be contented. But on the other hand, they should never succumb to satisfaction with the way things are in our world. I will often attempt to stir up a drive to accomplish more during my presidential charge at graduation:

> Like many of you, I have been a traditional student, finishing my bachelor's degree and my first master's degree when I was in my twenties. But like many others of you, I've also been a non-traditional student, first as an eighteen-year-old immigrant to the US, navigating visas and the INS, and then as a nontraditional student who went back to school in his forties to complete a second master's degree and a PhD while working full time with a wife and a flock of children.

> Graduates, like many of you, I was driven by a desire to better myself so that I could make a bigger impact. Most of us in this

room know, at one level or another, that deep-down, nagging sense of dissatisfaction.

It's that unsettling sense that we are meant for more. It moves us to dig in and be creative, to make something out of nothing. It drives us to be difference makers, especially for the sake of those we love. It pushes us to keep on keeping on, studying through tears, climbing through exhaustion, finishing what we started. And this you have done. So smile, showing all your teeth. Celebrate the moment! And as you close your eyes tonight, give thanks with a grateful heart filled to the brim with personal satisfaction. However, it is my hope that you will wake up on some not too far-off tomorrow, *dissatisfied* again, ready to shake up this messed-up world, a world with which we cannot in good conscience ever be fully satisfied. Dissatisfied with anti-Semitism. Dissatisfied with Islamophobia. Dissatisfied with the persecution of Christians globally. Dissatisfied with the corruption and dysfunction on both sides of the political aisle. Dissatisfied with the broken parts of our educational system and unjust aspects of our legal system. Dissatisfied with the epidemic of domestic gun violence and the pandemic of hopelessness leading to things like opioid abuse.

For today, be *satisfied*. We are so proud of you! But you are meant for more than resting on your diploma! I know this because you are Concordia—New Yorkers! And this world needs you to channel your justifiable dissatisfaction into the research laboratory to find a cure, into some hospital room, into the Wall Street executive suite, into your classroom, into the town hall meeting, onto social media platforms, into the voting booth, and maybe one of you all the way into the White House.

In conclusion, congratulations, graduates! And thanks in advance for all that your dissatisfaction will do to wake us up, to shake things up, and to make this planet a better place.

~~~~~~~~~~~~~~~~~~~~~

MERCIFUL GOD, YOU SAVE US BY SERVING US WITH YOUR GIFTS
OF GRACE. MAY JESUS' NAME KEEP US RESTLESS SO THAT YOU
MAY USE US IN SERVICE TO OTHERS. AMEN.

~~~~~~~~~~~~~~~~~~~~~

Jeremiah: A Restless Contemporary

The prophet Jeremiah suffered from this same restlessness, this same dissatisfaction. Travel back in time with me more than 2,600 years ago; you might recognize more of Jeremiah's situation than you'd think. In Jeremiah's day, powerful people cared more about their own profit than about people living in the margins or in poverty, ignoring God's clear Word to care for others and instead listening to false teachers. As Jeremiah said: "From the least to the greatest of them, everyone is greedy for unjust gain; and from prophet to priest, everyone deals falsely" (Jeremiah 6:13).

But Jeremiah was called by God (Jeremiah 1:5) to fight against these evils. Despite unpopularity, antipathy, and death threats, Jeremiah refused to tiptoe around God's truth; his sermons were chock-full of challenging words that got in the face and under the skin of those ignoring God's Word. He warned them that unless they turned around, they would be as "dead bodies . . . fall[ing] like dung upon the open field" (Jeremiah 9:22). These are not the kinds of words that win friends, influence people, or satisfy the status quo! Jeremiah sometimes reminds me of a howling backwoods blues singer, his harmonica wailing, his guitar strumming with the pain of these evils. Listen to these lyrics from his songbook: "My joy is gone; grief is upon me; my heart is sick. . . . Is there no balm in Gilead?" (8:18, 22). Jeremiah was stressed, distressed, fatigued, and fed up with what was going on around him.

JEREMIAH

Have you ever felt drained and down in the dumps by how tough it is to be a believer? "I have become a laughingstock all the day," Jeremiah cried out. "Everyone mocks me" (Jeremiah 20:7). Laughing at oneself? Usually a healthy sign of humility. Laughing mockingly at others? That's an unhealthy sign of arrogance or insecurity, but it doesn't make it hurt any less for those being laughed at.

This sounds like the same world you and I inhabit, and God has called us out and set us apart, in the church, with the promise: " 'Who can hide in secret places so that I cannot see them?' declares the LORD. 'Do not I fill heaven and earth?' declares the LORD" (Jeremiah 23:24 NIV). No matter what people think, there is a God who sits on high and yet looks low at those dwelling in valleys of the shadow of death. This God knows human suffering. This God is both aware of what is unfair and cares about injustice. The good news is if you're suffering today, there is no pain that God does not feel. The bad news is if you think that you're getting away with doing bad things today, the eyes of God are on you. There is no place you can hide from God. What you're currently going through will not define you in the eyes of your true friends, nor can it ever divide you from the love of God in Christ Jesus (Romans 8:38–39).

Almost fifty years ago, Arthur Carl Piepkorn wrote these timeless words: "In our era and in our culture . . . [with its] drift toward the demonic . . . [and its] flight from integrity toward disintegration and a centrifugal thrust toward undisguised nihilism, we need as the church to be able to affirm that our whole universe hangs together in Christ."[45]

In Christ alone, we stand strong! Like Jeremiah, we can become exhausted by the circumstances of life, but I believe in the Holy Spirit, the Lord and giver of life, who will fill our brokenness with wholeness, our regret with forgiveness, our sorrow with the joy of Jesus, our feelings of nothingness and hopelessness with seeing the goodness of the Lord in the land of the living (Psalm 27:13)!

Has sin left you with spiritual indebtedness? God has the perfect righteousness earned by Jesus with your name on it. "The LORD is our righteousness," Jeremiah declares (23:6). The same Jesus who was filled

---

45   Arthur Carl Piepkorn, "The One Eucharist for the One World," *Concordia Theological Monthly* 43, no. 2 (February 1972): 100, https://media.ctsfw.edu/Text/ViewDetails/9236.

with the fullness of God (Ephesians 3:19) in turn fills you and me with that same fullness so that we are no longer full of ourselves, no longer filling up on the rubbish of this world, but instead, we are full of "the surpassing worth of knowing Christ Jesus my Lord" (Philippians 3:8). As my friend David Scaer puts it: "Whereas Baptism places believers into Christ, the Eucharist places Christ into believers. Now that they're in Christ with Christ in them, these believers can't help but extend mercy to the 'Christ' in the least of those around them."[46]

We are set apart by Christ from our sandboxes of selfishness; we are set free for lives of selfless service. We may feel depleted and drained, but God is replete with power to fill you, overflowing in grace that bubbles over for you. You are baptized! You have the same promise God gave to Jeremiah: "I will deliver you out of the hand of the wicked, and redeem you from the grasp of the ruthless" (Jeremiah 15:21). You have been yanked from death to new life in three splashes of water, delivered by the Father, redeemed by the Son, and fully qualified to live out loud "in demonstration of the Spirit and of power" (1 Corinthians 2:4).

---

46   These comments were included in an email correspondence of April 11, 2005.

13

DISCERNING MORE

*W*hen Dr. Oswald Hoffmann, a former speaker for the *Lutheran Hour*, was once asked about a preacher, he said there were only three things wrong with the sermon: The preacher read it, he didn't read it well, and it wasn't worth reading. Sacred Scripture is always worth reading. So are labels. Reading is one thing. Discerning what one has consumed is quite another.

1. It sat so deceptively, so innocently, on the shelf, pretending to be the regular Listerine. I wasn't wearing my glasses.

2. Without any heads-up, Monique switched to a concentrated mouthwash with which I was unfamiliar—the dangerous impostor, Dr. Tichener's.

3. When it first entered my mouth, I thought it was a toxic industrial cleaning fluid.

4. Having thought I'd accidentally killed myself, I emitted a series of uncharacteristic squeals and did, in fact, perform an exuberant panic dance.

5. Monique assured me that it wouldn't be too long before my taste buds began working again.

6. From now on, I will read the label before using.

Discerning is not so simple. While I was on a flight to visit my widowed mother, a flight attendant droned on with the usual preflight instructions. Who listens? "Blah, blah, mask, blah, blah, these are the exits . . ." Then, she directly addressed those of us sitting in the exit row and requested a verbal response. She talked about performing certain tasks in case of an emergency, but when she concluded with this sentence, I sat up and paid attention: "If a nondiscernible condition should prevent you from completing the necessary functions, please let us know and you will be reseated." How, I wondered to myself, does one know whether she or he is the possessor of a nondiscernible condition—especially since "nondiscernible" implies the inability to discern it? But I wouldn't dare to ask her that.

Instead, I inquired, with metaphysical charm, of this flight attendant, "What constitutes a nondiscernible condition as contrasted with a discernible condition?"

"Are you a lawyer?" she asked me.

"I am not," I said, but in my mind, in a manner quite lawyerlike, I was contemplating the range of possibilities of my own personal, nondiscernible issues.

Then my mind roamed to my mother. After fifty-five years of marriage, my mother became a widow. She married my father at eighteen and has never known another man. Her grief will likely never be assuaged, though she appears to most who see her as normal, not suffering from any recognizable pain. Now, several years after losing her husband, her grief has concretized as a permanent, nondiscernible condition. The pain of losing her life partner scorched her soul. Having him wrenched from her life formed an ache she attempted to conceal, but it clutched her relentlessly as she limped her way through life.

What are other options for nondiscernible conditions? Some beneath-the-surface condition that nobody sees . . . Something in your personal past that nobody but God knows . . . Some financial anxiety that keeps you from sleeping at night . . . Some abuse that you cannot bear to reveal because of what it would do to people you love . . .

NEVILLE AND RUTH NUNES

Praying More

What can we do when we're dealing with our own nondiscernible conditions? What actions can we take? My mother has chosen praying.

Afraid? Worried? Anxious? Riddled with grief? Here's what to do and here's what will happen. It's an unsurprisingly ancient and time-tested solution: pray unceasingly and work tirelessly to combat your problem. The logical results are that either you will lose faith and be driven to despair or—if you don't give up, if you keep the faith—you will lose your fear and be driven to new heights, new levels where there's more to come. And here's the surprise they rarely tell you about: you will inevitably meet new devils when you rise to new levels. These are not to be feared. You know what overcoming them feels like, how the Word drives them away, and you know who ultimately has the victory over that terrible triad of sin, death, and the devil. So, work and pray. The principle is this: Those who rise in faith from their fear have risen with an unseen courage that comes from an unseen source, the risen Jesus who rules at the right hand of God and will return with a final judgment on everything that terrorizes us. The struggle is real, the warfare is difficult, but the devil is already defeated. This helps us to rise to the more for which we are meant in the midst of the anxiety and stress we face daily.

Another woman I overheard had a decidedly different way to deal with others as she evidently dealt with her own nondiscernible condition. Hearing her chastise the service station staff and random customers, "You, you, and you are working my nerves!" I thought to myself: when absolutely everyone around you is working your nerves, it could be an indicator that you yourself, not everyone else, need to do some spiritual work on your nerves.

> **For we do not wrestle against flesh and blood, but against the rulers, against the authorities, against the cosmic powers over this present darkness, against the spiritual forces of evil in the heavenly places. Therefore take up the whole armor of God, that**

you may be able to withstand in the evil day, and having done
all, to stand firm. (Ephesians 6:12–13)

For our actions to make a difference in ordinary lives—our own
and those we are called to impact—we need the traction to stand firm.
This derives not from our weak selves, but from a source that is in,
with, and under the ordinary, a source that is extraordinary, that is
from out of this world, because this source is the Creator, the Savior,
and the Sanctifier of this world.

A Nondiscernible Condition

We all carry around a fatal nondiscernible condition called *sin*.
And because of that big, three-letter word, there is some stuff in life
that is nondiscernible, indescribable, not intellectually solvable. We see
it when we face pain that seems unbearable. When we are controlled
by injustice that seems unbeatable. When we have an unfair amount
of stress on our overloaded plates. When we arrive at the horizon and
no way forward seems possible. When we're all cried out and we've
tried every option and nothing will give. When we've prayed until our
knees are bruised, our eyes are red, our voices are raspy, and we are
exhausted with the sort of fatigue that a single night's rest cannot cure.
If you're at the end of your rope, don't let go, don't give up, don't give
in. The end of your rope is a perfect place to practice the perfect peace
that comes with being still (Psalm 46:10). Being still means that even
if you're hanging by a thread, when you get to the end of your rope,
in faith, you tie a knot of hope and say, "Lord, have mercy," and say,
"Come, Holy Spirit," and say, "Your kingdom come. Your will be done."

God's Hand at Work

Faith is not a seat belt or a talisman or a magic formula or a good-luck
charm. As I write these words, I have two friends who are in hospice
care, Rev. Duane Geary and Paula Schlueter Ross. By the time your
eyes land on their names, they will certainly have transitioned. One is

black; one is white. One is a clergyman; the other is a laywoman. Both worked for the church for decades. Both were filled to the brim with faith in ways that led me to ask them the reason for their joy even in the face of a diagnosis of death. Both shared that they see the hand of God keeping them through this. One, from her deathbed, texted me these words: "I feel that God is directing even these things and has not abandoned me. In fact, God shows up many times during the day—in a helpful nurse, a caring doctor, messages and visits from friends."

Because of sin, we all have the unbeatable diagnosis of death, but Psalm 16:11 makes us this promise despite the cold, fatal hand that will one day grip us: "In Your presence there is fullness of joy." This joy gives us more strength than we could conceive (Nehemiah 8:10) for the backbreaking burdens we bear, burdens that are not only indescribable but often indiscernible. Often, the more we bear a calling, the more we hear a rationale for that vocation that is beyond human rationality or the comprehension of our companions. For example, I have grown in the certainty of my vocational commitment to lead and serve at Concordia College—New York despite the distresses and pressures of leadership. It's an arduous journey. When some aspiring college presidents from the ELCA and the LCMS asked me for advice, I suggested, "Whatever healthy ego you have, whatever sanctified self-confidence is yours, nurture that interior self and fill it with integrity. Because if you become a president, every bit of that will get squeezed out of you by the pressure of this job." But tough times bring clarity regarding one's calling and utter conviction in one's vocation.

Additionally, my faith has grown in God's unmeasurable goodness, which Martin Luther once described as often "unseen and unknown." Since we are God's *handiwork* we can be sure, in spite of what we see and feel, that behind the scenes, there is always a hand at work.

Cut through today's clutter, O God. Clear a path for me to discern more clearly, to hear again of Christ's unceasing love for me. Then guide me by Your Spirit to bear with sincerity that same love into the lives of others, especially those with whom that message does not happen easily. Do this, God, for the sake of all who limp their way through life. In Jesus' name. Amen.

Perceiving More

Ornamented with statues, gold-plated candlesticks, and faceted glass—such beauty drew our gazes to the One who is the source of all beauty. It was as if our eyes transported our hearts upward. The room in which I stood was obviously a place of solemnity—a church. This day, however, the space was buzzing, transfigured by 250 elementary-school-aged children clapping joyfully, singing with full-throated praise, praying as if they believed every word was being heard by God. As the morning chapel speaker, I smiled and made small talk with the children, chitchatting my way toward the front of the room, the speaker's place.

A reserved, studious eight-year-old, the sort of child who avoids eye contact, caught my eye.

"How are you?" I inquired.

"Very well," she replied with a firm tone, seemingly intent on ending the conversation.

So I quickly quipped, "I really like your glasses. The blue frames are cool. Do they help you to see better?"

"No, they don't," she surprisingly replied with pride. "They help me to see bigger, not better!"

Perhaps we all need those sorts of glasses. The kind of vision that helps us not to see better what's already there—there's too much bad stuff I don't need to see any better. But there's also too much good stuff, the small things, that I need to see bigger—especially the overlooked things, the least of these, the forgotten, the neglected, those who embody Jesus.

It hurts, heartbreakingly, to see the impact of sin on this world, doesn't it? So much pain on this planet. We're overexposed to a non-stop news cycle of negativity. We're overwhelmed in our own families with folks who share the same blood but cannot share a meal together without fighting to create their own version of Family Feud. We're augmented with anxiety and diminished by doubt about what we see, like the workplace shootings or the school shootings that have become so commonplace that to mention them feels cliché. Or the black and brown kids killed so frequently in street shootings that it doesn't even make the news anymore. Every time there's a warm weekend on the west or south side of Chicago, shootings erupt so predictably that they approach wartime levels—so much that Spike Lee made the movie *Chi-Raq* about them. Of course, it's not just Chicago, and it's not just large cities. The prophet challenges us to "seek the welfare of the city where I have sent you into exile, and pray to the LORD on its behalf, for in its welfare you will find your welfare" (Jeremiah 29:7).

Churches resound with triumphant songs, like "new hymns throughout the world shall ring," but we see the same old sins destroying us. Churches call out to God each week, "In peace, let us pray to the Lord," but our souls are restless. Churches hear the promise that we will receive power to be witnesses to the end of the earth (Acts 1:8)—wow! Yet we feel so powerless about what's happening beyond the end of our driveway, if that far. The more I see down here, no wonder those followers of Jesus were gazing up there to find any shred of hope (Acts 1:10–11).

We all need the relentless reminder of Paul encouraging us in Ephesians 1:18 that God is the enlightener of the eyes of my heart. Because of this promise, we can see rightly! As that occurs, it won't necessarily change *what* we see; rather, it changes *how* we see it. We see the same things, but in them, with them, and under them, we see the blessing of God. During the COVID-19 pandemic, New York City was one of the first epicenters in the US. I have a friend, Father Mike, whose Washington Heights parish lost more than forty members in the space of some forty days. With him in mind, I composed this responsive prayer:

> **ALL:** IN THE NAME OF THE FATHER AND OF THE SON AND OF THE HOLY SPIRIT. AMEN.
>
> **L:** STRONG AND LOVING GOD, IN OUR WILDERNESS, WE HEAR YOUR VOICE INVITING US TO TURN TO YOU.
> **R:** WE ARE WORN OUT.
> **L:** SUFFERING BLUDGEONS THE LAND!
> **R:** WE ARE DUST.
> **L:** AN ENEMY IS PURSUING US WITH DEATH.
> **R:** WE ARE TERRIFIED.
> **L:** YET FOR THIS PLANET, YOU HAVE A PLAN PULSATING WITH LIFE. REMOVE THE BLINDFOLDS OF FEAR FROM OUR SIGHT
> **R:** SO THAT WE MIGHT SEE THE SUNBURST OF YOUR SPIRIT.
> **L:** SHOW US YOUR VISION FOR DEALING WITH CRISIS.
> **R:** HEALING GOD, WE NEED YOUR HELP.
> **L:** CASCADE INTO OUR LIVES STREAMS OF NEW MEANING FROM THE WORDS IN YOUR WORD.
> **R:** MAKE US BOLD.
> **L:** OPEN OUR SENSES TO IMAGINE THE POSSIBILITIES FOR EMPATHY: FOR THOSE WHO HAVE LOST HOPE IN GETTING WELL,
> **R:** HAVE MERCY, LORD!
> **L:** FOR THOSE WHO KNOW FAR TOO WELL THAT THE ECONOMIC STRUGGLE IS REAL,
> **R:** HAVE MERCY, LORD!
> **L:** FOR ANGUISHED INDIVIDUALS SHRIVELING IN THE LONELINESS OF ISOLATION,
> **R:** HAVE MERCY, LORD!
> **L:** FOR STUDENTS NAVIGATING FOR THE FIRST TIME A STRANGE NEW WORLD OF SEEMINGLY SHRUNKEN OPPORTUNITIES,

R: Have mercy, Lord!

L: For families, at their wits' end, feeling stressed—out, blocked—in, and locked—down,

R: Have mercy, Lord!

L: You, O God, are a mighty rushing river of mercy;

R: Flow into our lives.

L: Animate us to be who we are,

R: the Body of Christ.

L: O God of the resurrection.

R: Raise us up.

L: Shatter the cocky carapaces we've acquired over the years as we humbly claim Your promises with childlike confidence.

R: In Your name, we pray:

L: the Deliverer from dangers seen and unseen and from diseases known and unknown;

R: In Your name, we pray:

L: the Bringer of both the bread of life and the breath of life;

R: In Your name, we pray:

L: our Emancipator whom we shall see one day, without any social distancing,

ALL: Jesus, our joy! Amen.

14

HOPING MORE

*A*few biblical words to frame these thoughts about hope. First, from Romans 8:24: "For in this hope we were saved. Now hope that is seen is not hope." And then four words from 1 Corinthians 13:7: "Love . . . hopes all things."

For some people, optimism about society is impossible because they see the world as an unfixable evil to be endured at best, and anyone different is to be shunned. For others, the social order is a perfectible goal to be pursued through the primacy of reason, the abandonment of passion, and the confidence of enlightened enjoyment—this, ironically, despite the culture's regression to spiritual despair, evidenced, in part, by some tragically choosing to commit suicide. In our time, I suggest that the world is a gift, like an icon, to be engaged—respectfully, carefully, caringly, discerningly because of sin, but reverentially since God loved it and gave Himself for it in Jesus Christ. We watch and wait, dialogue and debate, our eyes anticipating a beauty beyond the horizon of this life.

Yet, the impulse to leave this world may be part of the deep inner sense that we are meant for more. Consider the words of this African American spiritual: "And before I'd be a slave, I'd be buried in my grave, and go home to my Lord and be free." This sentiment differs little from Paul's dilemma: "I am hard pressed between the two. My desire is to depart and be with Christ, for that is far better" (Philippians 1:23).

In 1530, Martin Luther wrote to Jerome Weller, a young man struggling with spiritual depression.[47] I am exercising significant literary license to update four points in the letter:

> Dear Jerome (and reader),
>
> When the despair comes and kicks you in the backside, know that you are being attacked demonically because you belong to God. The devil doesn't attack those he already owns or can control.
>
> The best defense is to laugh in the devil's face. Why would you argue with a thing that loves arguing and twisting the truth? Don't dwell on it. Just laugh mockingly, show him the hand, remember you are baptized, tell him to scram, make the sign of the cross, and keep on walking because the devil is already defeated.
>
> Beware of being alone, detached from the Body of Christ. There is strength in numbers, encouragement in the fellowship. The devil waits to attack when we are hungry, angry, lonely, or tired. Beware of HALT.
>
> When the devil throws your sins in your face and reminds you that you have a bad past and says you don't deserve God's love, just say, "That's true, I probably deserve death and hell. But so what? May I introduce you to my great future in Jesus Christ, the Son of God, who died for me, gives me a forgiveness you wouldn't understand, and lives that I might live with Him forever."
>
> Yours truly,
>
> Martin Luther
> and his twenty-first-century protégé
> John Arthur Nunes

---

47 *Luther: Letters of Spiritual Counsel*, trans. and ed. Theodore G. Tappert (orig., 1960; reprint, Vancouver, BC: Regent College Publishing, 2003), 85.

First, love hopes all things. Hope will suffocate without a consistent infusion of God's love. It cannot breathe or stay alive if it tries to be independent of love. Disconnected from God's love, hope dies. Even when the evidence is stacked against it, hope can survive if it is rooted, grounded, planted, and motivated by God's miraculous, unconditional, no-strings-attached, no-hyperbole-too-large-for-this love in Jesus Christ. For you. For me. No love, no hope. No hope without love. Oh, that we would embrace more emphatically that we are deeply and undeservedly loved so that we might suffuse ourselves in this love that hopes all things.

Not that we are experts at love—the list is long of the people, places, and things I struggle to love—but that we are sacrificially loved by a love that bled, died, and was resurrected with fresh life for you and me.

Staying More Woke Means Keeping More Hope

This subtitle is awkward. Its clumsiness derives, in part, from attempting to honor "staying woke" as a term derived from African American communities. It refers to the need for keeping vigil, maintaining awareness, especially around topics of social justice and racism. I have suffered, my family has suffered, and I fear future suffering caused by racial injustice for my six children and (so far) eleven grandchildren. I agree with vigilance, and I also have two cautionary comments.

First, we must not live in fear nor live in anger. Being aware is healthy. There are liberal ways to be racist—for example, to quote a former US president, with "the soft bigotry of low expectations." There are also moderate ways to be racist, such as claiming not to see race, and conservative ways to be racist, such as cultural supremacism. There are, however, no theologically justifiable ways to be a racist Christian. So, on one hand, there is ample evidence of racialized oppression across the ideological spectrum (humans are, after all, catastrophically fallen); on the other hand, there is also something disordered with being hyperaware, preoccupied with the racist plot under every rock, a demonic, oppressor bogeyman behind every problem we face. At some point, those who are standing watch and staying woke need rest for their souls; Jesus invites and inspires us with His promise, "Come to Me . . . and I will give you rest" (Matthew 11:28).

My second cautionary comment is that, in the midst of awareness and wokefulness, people of Christian faith must never abandon hopefulness. The fullness of hopefulness in God isn't passive optimism. With grammatical and theological force, hope connects itself with the subject of the verb *love*. God is love. Love is the parent; hope is the offspring. God is the source, love is the root, and hope is the fruit! And hope gives birth to much more than we can begin to believe. My second point borrows from Robert McAfee Brown, who put it like this: "Hope has two beautiful daughters. One is anger and the other is courage. Anger—at what? Anger at the way things are. Courage—to do what? Courage to see that they do not remain the way they are."[48]

In other words, I believe that Christians are a positive people filled with hope, brimming with joy, overflowing with love, but that doesn't mean we are complacently satisfied with the status quo, smugly contented with the way things are. Constructing a hopefulness that is built on faulty assumptions often produces the opposite result: hopelessness. Just because I am a person of hope doesn't mean I am not animated with anger at the injustice, unfairness, institutional stupidity, structural oppression, and individual immorality that proliferates because of sin in the world and in the church. However, I do not live in anger—human anger is also prone to pride—I live in hope, which draws me toward hope's beautiful daughter named "courage," and she speaks to her beautiful sister "anger" and says, "Thanks for getting my attention and giving me the motivation to recognize evil; I am courage, here for you with power to take action, with our hopeful parent's promise, that we will make a difference, we will reverse the curse, reverse the death dive of despair, dare to do more to give people a peek of God's reign on earth."

---

48 Robert McAfee Brown, *Speaking to Christianity* (Louisville, KY: Westminster John Knox Press, 1997), 74. Brown credits Augustine with this comment but does not know where it is written in Augustine's works.

Encouraging More

Life is no game, yet knowing what's ultimate, what not to sweat, and how to hold all things in balance is a mark of mature faith that leads to a playful, bold, others-oriented, encouraging, and happy approach to life. In a world suffering from a deficit of joy, we dare to make the most of every opportunity to encourage others with the infinitely abundant joy Jesus gives us.

> HE WHO BINDS TO HIMSELF A JOY
> DOES THE WINGED LIFE DESTROY
> BUT HE WHO KISSES THE JOY AS IT FLIES
> LIVES IN ETERNITY'S SUNRISE.[49]

More Joy

During a transatlantic flight on the way home from international business with Lutheran World Relief, long after my mind had blurred by too much reading of my PhD course material, I found what I hoped to be mindless reprieve in the in-flight feature, *The Bucket List*. The lead characters are facing imminent death. (These roles, incidentally, are played dazzlingly by Jack Nicholson and Morgan Freeman.) So, they compose and then execute their list of things to do prior to "kicking the bucket." They drive fast cars. They skydive. They travel to exotic destinations. Upon arriving at the pyramids, the character played by Morgan Freeman muses on how ancients believed there would be two questions posed at the end of life, asking whether a person has found joy in their own life and whether they were able to bring joy to the lives of others. These queries have remained a self-critical filter for life since I first heard them, a way of keeping matters that matter most on the top of my personal priority list. How would I answer these questions? I'd say I have discovered joy, or better, I've been discovered by the joy

---

49   William Blake, "Eternity," Blake's Notebook.

of the Lord, the gift of grace that comes through my faith in Jesus. But the second question implies an action. Joy isn't for hoarding. We are nudged to consider how we use our resources to extend that joy to others—joy as a source of encouragement.

Joy matters to God. Martin Luther thought so too: "God is repelled by sorrow of spirit; He hates sorrowful teaching and sorrowful thoughts and words, and He takes pleasure in happiness. For He came to refresh us, not to sadden us. Hence the prophets, apostles, and Christ Himself always urge, indeed command, that we rejoice and exult."[50]

What happens when young people do not hear words of encouragement, words of hope? In the summer of 2018, chatter escalated on social media. Traffic was blocked in my wife's former neighborhood because of the report of a death near Chicago's Dan Ryan Expressway (I-95). Commentators immediately began to hypothesize that this must surely be another shooting. No. A sixteen-year-old girl just jumped in front of a Red Line CTA train. On this sunny, summer Saturday, this child decided she had no more reason to live. Sure, we must pray more for our children, but especially, we must *do* more to give them health and hope. Life is no game. Death is final when there is no hope.

---

50 *LW* 27:93.

Upon hearing of this specific story on June 23, 2018—it was a Saturday as Monique and I flew on Delta Flight 2518 from Detroit to Orlando—that I sent a text message proposal for this book to Concordia Publishing House president and CEO Dr. Bruce Kintz. Certainly, lives are meant for more than the extraordinary pain too many people are crushed by, leading to these sorts of tragic endings.

Just because you're having a bad day doesn't mean you are doomed or destined to have a bad life any more than a lifeless tree in the dead of winter means there is no future promise. Life is seasonal. That's why we stay connected to the lifeline of bread and wine and the daily reminder of Baptism. These Sacraments provide the objective assurance that God's good things are *for you* today and that you are not without hope or joy to be seen on some tomorrow, either in this sphere of existence or the next. In 2007, I was a forty-something-year-old husband, father, and CEO of a large nonprofit, and I was also in pursuit of my PhD. There were more days than anyone knows when I felt the load of it all would break me. But God always sent a breakthrough that I wouldn't have recognized without the eye-opening preparation of suffering. Overcoming challenges. Facing obstacles. Struggling against seemingly impossible impediments. We do not fight alone. We have the promise of God's overcoming presence.

I met David Stern once, in 2009. He was compassionate and wise as he represented the National Basketball Association and their efforts to end malaria called "Nothing But Nets." Lutheran World Relief was launching the Lutheran Malaria Initiative. In a sidebar conversation, I asked him, "What do you tell these young boys who think they're going to play in the NBA?" His reply: "Tell them about a short, twelve-year-old Jewish kid from New York City who wanted to play professional basketball. His teacher told him to focus on his education. So that's what he did, and now I run the NBA."

We all have something in our lives to overcome. We all have someone in our lives to encourage. But in the face of all that we face, in all that confronts us, take this to heart: you possess a way-above-the-rim capacity realizable in Jesus Christ. In Romans 8:37, we are described in Christ as *hyper* ("above") *nike* ("victor"). We are more than conquerors through the One who loved us more than we can imagine. That's more than encouraging—it's courage-giving.

WHERE THERE'S A WILL TO COMMUNICATE, THERE'S ALWAYS A WAY.

15

COMMUNICATING MORE

efore ordering the avocado salad at a Chinese restaurant in New York City, I had a question. Unfortunately, neither I nor the server, Jason, understood each other's language enough to get an answer to "What kind of greens do you use for the salad?" After darting into the kitchen, he returned with a sample that made me smile—in his hand, a plate with a single leaf of romaine lettuce.

Where there's a will to communicate, there's always a way. It seems like we are more prone to communicate our agitations, irritations, and expectations than we are to communicate our encouragement and common humanity.

In the past fifty years, academic communities and faith communities have improved in their intellectual responsibility to scrutinize bigotries, examine injustices, challenge orthodoxies, and unearth ignored histories. These are among the duties of thought leaders in a free society. What we haven't been as good at is welcoming differences of opinion to that work (within the bounds of reasoned research and respectful dialogue). Our world needs academic and faith communities that both respect the enduring progress worked by institutions and also promote individual freedoms. What if we owned this two-pronged obligation? What if we, as citizens, contributed, sacrificed, gave back to our communities with as much vigor as we assert our own individual rights to expect access to opportunities? What if mercy toward neighbor mattered as much as fighting for justice for ourselves, for our own kin, and for our own kind? What if long-lasting traditions were as protected and highly regarded as the latest, shiny trends? What if we paid as much attention to *them* as we do to *us*? What if we were as generously open to various spectra of perspective at the same time that we provided space for reasonable and respectful counterarguments? It's hard to find a good, fair debate when we're lobbing epithets and constructing stereotypical strawmen. We need rules of engagement and safe spaces to communicate. We are meant for more. We need a new movement in the USA, where people can come together to discuss real problems with real people face-to-face, in a respectful marketplace of ideas.

Too many good people hide within an electronic echo chamber rather than engage in face-to-face conversation. This amplifies our digital divide and erodes our sense of community—turning good people into shockingly bad people. Maybe we should fund a prize to recognize individuals who actively seek the high road in their interactions with others, those who pay attention to the integrity of their information first, and then communicate with civility and positivity.

When blustering self-confidence replaces personal character as the publicly rewarded trait of choice, we shouldn't be surprised to see people—especially our students—walking away from civility, giving up on critical thinking, and trading in their principled commitments to plume themselves instead with the feathery and foolish self-flattery of peacocks. Bravado does not facilitate the communication for which we were meant.

Witnessing More

For Christians, engaged and thoughtful communication is essential. Once you realize that you've been made righteous—that is, as a gift *from* God, you've been made right *with* God—you want to act in sharing that fact. Like good water flowing from a fresh source, Christians become talkative about their faith, using a conversational approach, winsome and whimsical, and treating the other as an end, not as a means to get another notch in the witnessing belt, another tick on the Christian-making clicker. But just because we engage in dialogue doesn't mean witnessing is timid or tepid or will not lead to trouble.

John the Baptist faced his share of trouble by striving to be a witness to the truth. (If you don't know much about him, read Luke 3:1–20.) What can we learn about speaking truth from the ministry of this uncivilized, grasshopper-eating, Jesus-teaching, tax-collector-baptizing, camel-hair-wearing, full-throttled, eschaton-preparing, name-calling ("you bunch of slick snakes" [see Luke 3:7]), Isaiah-echoing, fire-repentance-propheteering, field-preaching outsider who came out of the backcountry to stir things up in respectable religious society?

1. Speaking God's truth is often an unpopular, solitary activity; don't be surprised when you feel horribly alone, alienated, like an alien voice crying in the wilderness (Luke 3:4). This suffering should be unsurprising: "Indeed, all who desire to live a godly life in Christ Jesus will be persecuted" (2 Timothy 3:12). The truth sets free, as Jesus said; however, as one devout, active, lifelong Lutheran nonagenarian from Wisconsin put it, "But first, it's gonna tick off a whole bunch of people."

2. When they are attacked, truth speakers must avoid the twin temptations that arise on the spectrum of self-consciousness—on the one side is the paralyzing self-righteousness of being right, and on the other is the traumatizing self-pity of being victimized. And even if you remain even-headed about your suffering, you could still end up beheaded (Luke 9:9)! The only way to avoid these temptations is through prayerful self-reflection in the Word of God.

3. Similar to the in-filling of valleys, leveling of mountains, straightening of crooked ways, and smoothing over of rough places (Luke 3:5), truth speakers often use metaphors, poetry, or the indirectness of vivid analogies to convey their message.

4. Truth speakers stir up the established in-circle with diversity so that all flesh sees the salvation of God. In John's case, that meant both Jews and Gentiles. In our case, that means both those who are the likely and outwardly obvious candidates

for sainthood and those who might seem too ungifted, too unqualified, and too illegitimate to belong to St. Legitimate Lutheran Church.

"If you haven't found a cause worth dying for, you may not have found a reason worth living for." This is a paraphrase of Martin Luther King Jr.'s famous adage that I once heard in a homily. To be a witness is related to the Greek New Testament word *martyr*. John the Baptist gave his life for his Lord, literally having his head served on a platter. Not only should faith inevitably lead to witnessing, but it also could lead to becoming a martyr. Our lives of witness point to Jesus, the One who found someone worth dying for—you and me. His purposeful death gives us a reason to live, a cause to die for, and an irrevocable promise. Hear it in His own words: "'I am the Alpha and the Omega, the first and the last, the beginning and the end.' Blessed are those who wash their robes, so that they may have the right to the tree of life and that they may enter the city by the gates" (Revelation 22:13–14).

March 7 is designated by many Christians as a day of commemoration for two African women, Perpetua and Felicity, as well as their companions, martyred in AD 203 for being Christians. They shed their blood as a testimony to the One who gave His lifeblood as a salvific testament for all. Only in their twenties, these young converts to Christianity were starved, tortured, and finally killed for their faith. But since their robes were washed in the blood of the Lamb, in the name of the One who is the Alpha and the Omega, they "have the right to the tree of life" (Revelation 22:14). They are witnesses we rightfully remember, even emulate. Their faith has stood the test of time.

There are twenty-four letters in the Greek alphabet; alpha is the first, omega the last. These letters symbolize the function of Christ as the One in whom all things hold together. "'Who can hide in secret places so that I cannot see them?' declares the LORD. 'Do not I fill heaven and earth?' declares the LORD" (Jeremiah 23:24 NIV). There is no place that God is not present, no unsupervised suffering in the universe, no affliction that is outside of God's healing grace. This is good news for those who suffer for the faith as they strive to be witnesses. This also is bad news for those who cause the faithful to suffer insuperably.

SINCE THEY ARE WASHED IN THE BLOOD OF THE LAMB, IN THE NAME OF THE ... ALPHA AND THE OMEGA, "THEY HAVE THE RIGHT TO THE TREE OF LIFE." (REVELATION 22:14), THEY ARE WITNESSES WE RIGHTFULLY REMEMBER. ... THEIR FAITH HAS STOOD THE TEST OF TIME.

PERPETUA AND FELICITY

As one Lutheran theologian described it: "Christ Himself is the great hoop that circles the universe, the great parenthesis and bracket that unifies the diversity of things."[51] The righteousness of all those who suffer is earned by this Christ Jesus, who suffered even for the sake of those who cause suffering. Strangely, our trials, our tough times, and our troubles are meant to be more than mere suffering for us. They transform us as we witness from our weakness, giving praise to our Alpha and Omega, who encircles us and those we love with His endless love.

Not for Lutherans Only | PART 3

And yet, while acknowledging the suffering we face, the Lutheran faith is sometimes a bit too minor key for me. I get it that we are heirs of Martin Luther, but come on! Our instinct rightly distrusts theologies of glory; as a matter of principle, we are suspicious of stories of success, but rather than walking by faith *through* the valley of the shadow of death, we sometimes seem to dwell there, as residents of despair.

There was once among Lutherans in North America the strong perception of a confident intellectual vivaciousness, animated by a hopeful, theonomous worldview, not only embracing but leading in many public conversations and actions from the humanities to humanitarianism. Relative to their involvement in church and society, Lutherans nowadays seem to have lost their nerve and their identity. By which I mean, no Lutheran church body views their voice—when it consists of a distinctly Lutheran tone—as influential in the public square. The Lutheran loss of confidence is both a result and a cause of the bilateral Lutheran moves to two types of fundamentalism—one is retrogressive, the other is progressive.

"What has Athens to do with Jerusalem?" the ancient North African Tertullian probed. His answer, and that of many for centuries, is a resounding "Nothing!" For hundreds of years, Lutheranism, at its best, redefined its answer to that question with a characteristic paradox. There are, in tension, two realms in which God's hands are at work; one is Athens (or Rome), in creation, in science, in politics, in the secular

---

51   Arthur Carl Piepkorn, "The One Eucharist for the One World," *Concordia Theological Monthly* 43, no. 2 (February 1972): 100, https://media.ctsfw.edu/Text/ViewDetails/9236.

world. The other is Jerusalem, in the church, through the Gospel. These two are never to be separated from one another. Lutherans honor, on a practical level, the creative, First Article activity of God operative in Athens as well as the saving, Second and Third Article activity at work in Jerusalem. Such dual recognitions come easier when the general culture tends to enmesh Athens and Jerusalem. For example, in the late 1950s, all Lutherans composed about 4 percent of a US population that was 85 percent white. Franklin Clark Fry of the Lutheran Church in America was on the front cover of *Time* magazine, which called him "Mr. Protestant." Oswald Hoffmann was *Lutheran Hour* speaker and head of the LCMS Public Relations office in New York City. Lutheran church bodies were relatively well-known, possessed influence, and had access to seats of power. The demographics have shifted significantly in the twenty-first century. All Lutherans now compose less than 2 percent of the US population. Soon, whites will be a minority of US residents, and Lutherans are more white and more English-speaking than even Mormons, who had laws against minority participation.[52]

Basically, the loss of Lutheran confidence is both a result and a cause of this loss of Lutheran influence. Some express this loss of confidence by jettisoning Jerusalem. To jettison means to throw something overboard from a ship, a plane, or some form of craft. Those who jettison Jerusalem become increasingly indistinguishable from secular culture and tend to interpret theology primarily in ways that accommodate their cultural, socioeconomic, and political priorities. Their witness to Jesus as Savior from personal sinfulness (not merely societal sin) is sublimated. The other side anathematizes Athens. They become increasingly sectarian, see culture, science, and social advancement as an enemy, and tend to interpret theology in retrogressive terms, attempting to repristinate some earlier, often fairy-tale era of purity.

Rabbi Jonathan Sacks suggests that the story of Jeremiah is instructive. He neither withdrew, anathematizing Athens, nor assimilated, jettisoning Jerusalem. Rather he says, "Build houses and live in them; plant gardens and eat their produce. . . . Seek the welfare of the city where I have sent you into exile, and pray to the LORD on its behalf, for in its welfare you will find your welfare" (Jeremiah 29:5–7).

---

52 Data taken from the US Census Bureau (1952, 1961, and 2019 statistics), *The 2019 Lutheran Annual* (Concordia Publishing House), and ELCA statistics published on their website.

16

WORKING MORE

here is little to no correlation between increasing your workload and improving your life. It's obvious that making more money does not mean finding more meaning in life. What's less obvious is that meaning actually comes as a by-product of prioritizing people; we realize what is truly significant in life when we give thanks for those whom God has placed at our table rather than itemizing the commodities or assets we are lacking. Realizing who we are—recognizing our identity—helps us to work more for what matters and for those who matter.

A Piece of Work

To cite Shakespeare's *Hamlet*:

> **What a piece of work is a man! how noble in reason! how infinite in faculties! . . . in action how like an angel! in apprehension how like a god! the beauty of the world, the paragon of animals! And yet to me what is this quintessence of dust?[53]**

Often when I'm preaching or speaking, I enjoy modeling interaction. Occasionally, I ask those present to look at a human being nearby; if

---

53   Shakespeare, *Hamlet*, act 2, scene 2, lines 1397–1402, https://www.opensourceshakespeare.org/views/plays/play_view.php?WorkID=hamlet&Scope=entire&pleasewait=1&msg=pl.

that human being looks back and you make eye contact, tell them, "You're different." If they smile, tell them, "You're *really* different!" Saying this will often ease the room, create connections, and ready people to listen. Difference is a good thing; it's God's thing. It's what God built into the world. We are all pieces of work, but thank God we are God's pieces of work, and if you're God's piece of work, then you are a masterpiece of creation.

At every Mass, every Divine Service, every liturgy, hundreds of millions of Christians every Lord's Day profess their faith using the words of one of the ancient Ecumenical Creeds. "I believe in God, the Father Almighty, _____ of heaven and earth." The word in the blank is either *Maker* or *Creator*; it is translated from the Greek word *poet*. You are a masterpiece of the divine Poet of creation. Be the fullness of what you are.

Too often we find this identity hard to embrace. We don't feel like masterpieces. We don't feel loved unconditionally. And really, we are *not* accepted unreservedly by this world. We are *not* forgiven with no strings attached. We only get that in the world of the Gospel, and tragically, sometimes not even in church.

Picture the most grotesque situation you've ever been in, when you were caught red-handed. Perhaps it's a clandestine guiltiness known only to you and God. When God's love sees this situation, it doesn't run or retreat from it, but gets involved, gets engaged. "What wondrous love is this" that takes down-to-earth action for my sake. This love isn't a pie-in-the-sky, feel-good emotion, separated from the harsh realities of human experience. God's love takes action for us. God's love is documentable and demonstrable: Love, born in a barn in backwater Bethlehem. Love, bleeding for us on a cross of sacrifice. Love, dead and buried, but bursting back to life again to greet us. "Christ is risen," we shout!

Fast Work vs. Slow Work

Some personal stories are not helpful to tell publicly or publish in a book—at least, not until a safe amount of time has elapsed and you have everyone's permission. Then, and only then, do you carefully step out on the ledge to share hard-to-tell stories. The distinction between a wound and a scar is real. A wound is yet fresh, open, painful; a scar, while a visible reminder of pain, has begun the process of healing, one that is never completed in this life.

From roughly the year 2000 until 2010, when Monique and I became empty-nesters, back when our kids still ruled our roost, we would load up the SUV and truck our way over to Arcadia, Michigan, every summer with anywhere from three to six children in tow. Well, not like we were towing them, since they were inside the vehicle, but considering the spiritual quality of our destination, I must admit that there were some considerably unspiritual qualities on our journey to camp. For example, I do not recall a single visit in which we did not participate in our yearly ritual that I'll just call the Nunes Family Feud. While this was no game, it was quite a show. Like many overworked families, ours ordinarily lived through the year in dispersion, with us running in many different directions to and from myriad activities. So, this precious time together in the cramped quarters of the car provided a rare opportunity: togetherness! A time to air grievances—some of which had been suppressed, silenced, or stewing for months. Now that it's only Monique and I inhabiting the empty nest, we've had a decade of tranquil travel, with Mrs. Nunes ordinarily assuming the sleeping position. I have photographs to prove it.

But back in the day, we had an SUV full of kids hot as fish grease—not in temperature, but in temperament. One time it got so severe, I threatened to turn the vehicle around. When I firmly announced this to my passengers, my warning did absolutely nothing to stop the fussing and fighting, so I made a U-turn, which served to pump up the volume and led to me being told, in summary, that there wasn't a single dysfunction in my family for which I, their father, was not actually to blame. So, I pulled the vehicle over and went for a long walk to give these people the Lord had blessed me with some time to cool down. When I returned to the car, they were still there, waiting in stunned silence, so I drove to camp with nobody muttering a word. After about twelve hours to complete what should have been a five-hour trip, we arrived, all smiles, the pastor and his picture-perfect family.

I actually have looked back and thought hard about why our journeys to this piece of paradise called Arcadia were often marked with humans barking and biting at one another. I believe it's because a unique stress arises whenever humans are attempting to destress, striving to move from the day-to-day grind of fast work to a retreat-center pace of slow work, which, as I will attempt to demonstrate, is harder by far. That task of decompressing together is indescribably tough when we're with people we love deeply but haven't had the time, in our fast-work world, to do the slow work of talking about our hurts, our hopes, our private hells. Not until we all packed ourselves into the SUV for that road trip and were pressed together in a small space did we realize this.

No Spoilage

While the GPS could lead us to our destination, it couldn't help us navigate the transition from the fast-work tempo lived at the speed of life, from the day-to-day treadmill of shuttling kids to sports and music lessons and sleepovers, from the rat race of closing deals and paying the bills, chasing around to doctors and dentists and vets for the dogs. It's not easy to transition from all of that to the Sabbath of "slow work." Life confronts us with so many responsibilities, deadlines, calendar alerts, worthy causes and worthwhile busyness, stressors and pressures demanding our attention, summoning our attentiveness. In the face of all of this, we are masters of a skin-deep peace. As I mentioned earlier, a literary friend—who shall remain anonymous—reported his situation with these words: "My world consists of concentric circles of performance, masquerades. While some degree of theatrical fakeness is necessary to survive—authenticity can become a bloody mess—when there is no escape valve, people explode in stupidity. In the circle that's closest to you, you need something that's real and respectful, intimate and forgiving, sometimes even stupidly playful. Without it, you die of artificiality and artifice. You are a human, after all, very human."

Because this SUV was filled with flawed humans in close relationship and close proximity—starting with the driver, me—the sequestered travel to Arcadia became an "escape valve" or a release valve, maybe. Feelings that simmered, unaddressed, beneath the surface all year, family members feeling neglected, relationally malnourished, emotionally starved, undervalued, underprioritized because of the fast-work frenzy and the high-tech flash of trying to get ahead on the real freeway of life.

As I look back, I think I've learned that some of life's most worthwhile experiences cannot be executed efficiently, cannot be scheduled, are not integrated into a strategic plan. Things like extending forgiveness when your heart's been broken by betrayal, or that sparkle of pride in your child's eyes when she finally finishes her homework. If you're doing life as slow work, it's things like the elation of watching your vegetable garden grow, getting your hands dirty in life's slow work even when it's hard, even when it hurts. Slow work often yields unpredictable results with immeasurable blessings.

Jesus said: "Do not work for food that spoils, but for food that endures to eternal life, which the Son of Man will give you" (John 6:27 NIV). Just to clarify my categories, fast work is working for food that spoils, as Jesus says, and slow work is working for food that lasts. We can fool some people some of the time with our plastic images in a fast-work world, especially our so-called friends on social media. But we can't fool none of the people none of the time who know us and love us in our slow-work lives. With family or close friends or people we live with, it can't be faked; that's why it's really hard. But this is the food that lasts, and that matters!

Fast work praises moneymaking and getting promotions, building your resume without concern for the harm to fellow humans or the degradation to the environment. Slow work praises the Creator even when there is no ROI. So, if you want more from life, slow down; slow down and listen to the rhythm of the Spirit breathing between the words of Scripture, walking with you in difficult personal relationships, working with you as you pursue your calling. Slow down and listen for what Isaiah describes: "the mountains and the hills will burst into song . . . , and all the trees . . . will clap their hands" (55:12 NIV). Slow down and listen to what David describes: "Let the heavens be glad, and let the earth rejoice; let the sea roar [or at least the pond, lake, or marsh that's close to you] . . . ; let the field exult. . . . Then shall all the trees . . . sing for joy" (Psalm 96:11–12). Creation work is slow work. Wherever I've worked, I've often asked my direct reports whether they had any plants, kids, or pets. All three teach us patience through slow work, that we're not really in control, and that living things won't

THE MOUNTAINS AND HILLS WILL BURST INTO SONG, THE TREES CLAP THEIR HANDS

survive without nurture, all of which is as good for the giver as it is for the recipient.

Slow work isn't working slowly. Rather, it means to pace yourself, at least for a preplanned slice of life, with a panoramic reflectiveness. Slow work is circumspect, looking around, paying attention to these people with whom you are blessed, seeing the threads of the divine being woven through the seemingly scattershot arc of our all-too-common, often-too-boring, but certainly all-too-complicated lives. It cultivates a thoughtfulness about patterns. As my friend Barry Bobb might put it, "How does the soundtrack of my soul intersect with the songs of hope lived out loud among people I love?" Slow work is reflective. It might ask, "How does the day of my Baptism connect with how I want to be remembered at the end of my earthly life?" Answers to questions like these don't arrive with haste.

No Work

We all fail in finding the balance between fast work and slow work. We all fail in working for the food that lasts into eternal life. But the hardest work of all is neither fast nor slow; it's the no work that comes when one accepts the saving work that God has already accomplished. The no work that says it is by grace you have been saved through faith, not of your works. The no work that arrives in our eardrums with a shock, a language we could not possibly comprehend: we reap what we did not plant, we are paid for what we could not earn, we get what we did not give, we are forgiven for sins we forgot we'd ever done, we are rewarded for work we never had the good sense to even start to do, all because of the work that Jesus did, all almost impossible to accept, because humans are designed to work!

The work of engaging the Word, however, is that of the Spirit. Not to be too coarse, but shutting up and listening up might be the best approach to letting the living Word come to us in the stereophonic sound of Law and Gospel. You are loved and you are saved, not because you are particularly lovable or huggable or cute and cuddly in your injustice and selfishness or even because your family has fewer family feuds than the Nuneses. No, you are acceptable to God because of Jesus. No work! No human work could turn the pitiful pittance of two fish and five loaves of bread into an abundance, a feast for one of the world's biggest outdoor picnics.

In the very body and blood, in the ordinary bread and wine, Jesus Christ is not only the Lamb of God who works to take away the sin of the world, but Jesus also works to give us something in exchange for what He takes away. What a countercultural irritant this Jesus was to the imperial dreams of the Roman Empire and to all the self-made empires we work hard to construct! Imagine any politician running on a no-work economic platform. Only God could—and should, for that matter—work like that! It's a mind-popping mystery: all of us who believe in and are baptized into this no-work religion will crave after every scrap of chance we get to do good works because it is God who is at work in us, counting on us to be the justice-talking, humble-walking, mercy-loving, hardworking people of God.

17

MORE REDEMPTION?

o! Not only is there nothing we can do to warrant or deserve God's gift of redemption, there is nothing we can do to become *more* redeemed. What we *can* do is engage in practices that help us to realize more the gift we've been given. We begin with the Word of the Lord: "For I know that my Redeemer lives, and at the last He will stand upon the earth. And after my skin has been thus destroyed, yet in my flesh I shall see God, whom I shall see for myself, and my eyes shall behold, and not another. My heart faints within me!" (Job 19:25–27).

If an individual in Old Testament times was in any danger of being ousted from the family by war, hardship, or death, a redeemer was another family member who would pay a ransom, provide money for rescue or recovery, in order to secure the vulnerable member's membership in the group.

But this text points to more than just an independent, impersonal Redeemer. The "my" before "Redeemer" is personal, possessive, proprietary, and particular. It implies ownership and relationship. It is an intimate and proximate declaration. This proximity matters because it points to the presence of God. This is a connective annexation.

When the promises of God are annexed to the liturgical ceremony, a sacrament happens. When the promises of God are annexed to the ears of those who hear the preached Word, faith happens. When the promises of God are annexed to absolution, forgiveness happens. You can lay claim to your Baptism because when plain water and God's

Word are annexed to each other, the promises that God produces in that annexation are meant for you. This body and blood are for you because in, with, and under these elements is annexed the very presence of Jesus. He is personal, forever annexed to your life!

Punctuated More

New life in Christ is a once-for-all event. We are redeemed like a punctuating exclamation mark. It happened on the bloody Friday afternoon of Jesus' execution on a cross. Redemption is imprinted on every individual's watery death to sin in Baptism and is seized by every believer who by faith receives the free redemption of God; while the payday for sin is death, the promises of Christ's work have benefits for this life and the next (John 10:10; Romans 6:23). Jesus' sacrificial death and victorious resurrection is for us! Theologically speaking, this is seamless, simultaneous, and instantaneous.

But redemption is also a process. Life in the Spirit and the enjoyment of salvation's surplus represent an eye-opening pathway to ongoing redemption. Or as the catechism puts it, the Holy Spirit works through Word and Sacraments to "enlighten" us—which in Luther's German literally means "to turn on the light." What Christ did for us constitutes a once-for-all event, but humans often take an extended period of time to comprehend, apprehend, and appropriate the enormity of that redemption.

The Redeemer, the One who personalized love (as "my Redeemer"), becomes our salvation and then, by the Spirit, sends us out to those who are vulnerable, to those who have been ousted from their family, their community, or even society.

This Redeemer makes us resurrection revolutionaries. We love Easter because it assures us that we are meant for more than the grave. As such, our days are lived by faith in the echo of Easter. We know a resurrection that revolutionized the world. Few were there on Good Friday, and even fewer on the first Easter. Resurrection revolutions rarely go viral on social media. But resurrection revolutionaries know that Facebook is no replacement for face-to-face dialogue; they run from the deadly tomb of stereotypes (see chapter 8), witnessing life to

Joe the plumber, Jane the professor, Juan the immigrant, single moms working their way uphill through life's many-sided complexities.

Yes, we love Easter, but I am also a Pentecostophile—a lover of Pentecost. Martin Luther took to task those who didn't preach the whole trajectory of the Christian story: "They may be fine Easter preachers, but they are very poor Pentecost preachers. . . . Christ did not earn only *gratia*, 'grace' for us, but also *donum*, 'the gift of the Holy Spirit,' so that we might have not only forgiveness of, but also cessation of, sin."[54] He was aiming at Lutherans who so loved preaching and teaching about the Easter theme of the gift of salvation given by Jesus that they missed the Pentecost theme of the Spirit and spiritual gifts, also given by Jesus! The resurrection of Jesus is indeed the pinnacle of our salvation story, but it's not the end of the story.

The only way faith can grow is through the power of the Spirit working through Word and Sacraments. We need help, and we need the Helper. "I believe that I cannot by my own reason or strength believe in Jesus Christ; . . . but the Holy Spirit has called me . . . enlightened me . . . sanctified [me]," that is, made me holy (Luther's Small Catechism, explanation of the Third Article). And listen to Jesus' promise: "These things I have spoken to you while I am still with you. But the Helper, the Holy Spirit, whom the Father will send in My name, He will teach you all things and bring to your remembrance all that I have said to you" (John 14:25–26).

He, the Holy Spirit—not an *it* or a *thing*, but a Person of the Trinity—He "will teach [us] all things" (John 14:26). In his commentary on this passage, Martin Luther suggests that part of the ongoing work of the Holy Spirit is to "emphasize" the Word of God in ways that "make it clearer from day to day" so that we know Jesus increasingly better.[55] The Holy Spirit guides us in ways that enlighten us, opening our eyes to God's plan for all people, liberating us from sin and death. The truth of God is unchangingly transcendent, but our apprehension and understanding of that truth grows during our faith journey. We come to realize the new things that God is doing in our world, but only to the extent that we remain connected, not to the world, but to

---

54   *LW* 41:114.

55   *LW* 24:175.

the vine, Jesus. And we remain connected to Jesus Christ only to the extent that we do not block the work of the Spirit, who "will teach [us] all things."

More from Martin Luther: "We who have Christ are holy before God and have the Holy Spirit with us in opposition to any self-styled holiness."[56] How might we define "self-styled holiness" in North American churches in our time? Consider asking a friend who's outside of the faith, "How do forms of 'self-styled holiness' keep you from connecting with a church?" What aspects of Christianity might youth and young adults consider inauthentic faith? What would it take for them to give the church a chance? Consider the ways in which the Holy Spirit has changed your thinking about what God's Word says and, what's more, in the category of tradition.

We are pieces of work who too often forget our maker. "Who then can be saved?" Jesus' followers gasped with doubt (Matthew 19:25). Humans have a well-documented history of exploring political possibilities that eventually disintegrate in a bloodbath of disappointment, or of surfing an ocean of enlightened philosophies only to drown in an unpromising puddle of futility, or of probing the vast globe for mystical insights only to become entangled again in a cul-de-sac of despair. If history offers any lesson, it's that we cannot save ourselves, but as Jesus redirects us, "With God all things are possible" (Matthew 19:26). God accomplished what we could not, our salvation, by sending Jesus to close the sin-gap. Sin is terminal, the fatal flaw in humanity ever since Adam and Eve. Since Eden, we are incarcerated by sin and cannot free ourselves.

Liberation arrives only via (what I call) God's happy trade deal for humans. We get the lavish love of Jesus Christ in exchange for our slavish lovelessness. We get the love of Jesus Christ even while we are haters who seem to love to hate. We get His deep love that cannot die for our deeply disturbed loves of the things of the flesh that lead to death. We get His great faithfulness for our pettiness and unfaithfulness. His baptismal washing of our shame for our wishy-washy shamefulness. His righteousness for our fickleness of faith. His uprightness for our downright guiltiness. His justice for all of us for all of our human

---

56 *LW* 24:177.

injustices. The Spirit's unshakable integrity for our wobbly, willy-nilly lack of principle. Jesus' amazing grace for all of our unamazing lack of awesomeness. Jesus was forsaken by God—dying a death devoid of divinity on the cross—in our place, and in exchange, we get His promise never to leave us or forsake us, not ever! We get joy in exchange for despair, perfect peace for my anger, pardon for my death sentence, and finally, a resurrection to eternal life. All this because Jesus Christ is the Lamb of God, who not only takes away the sin of the world but also gives us something great in exchange for the sin He takes away. He gives us the faith that saves us and the power of the Spirit, who enables us to do good in the world.

So, are good works necessary? We might ask, "Necessary for what?" The answer is both yes and no. No, as is often ascribed to Martin Luther: God doesn't need your good works, but your neighbor does. Yes, your family does, your neighbor does, your congregation does, and your nation does! As the saying goes, "We are saved by faith alone, but faith is never alone." Faith alone? Yes and no. Faith is made possible by Scripture alone. Scripture shows us our Savior as Jesus Christ alone. Jesus has shown up in our lives because of grace alone, and grace always has a face . . . yours and mine doing good works in the world to the glory of God alone.

Not for Lutherans Only | PART 4

When it comes to this topic of good works, we're good at the Ephesians 2:8–9 part. We are good at knowing how we are saved. By what? Grace. Through what? Faith not works; salvation is the gift of God. No reason to boast! That's the upside of being Lutheran. The downside is that nobody is potentially lazier at being a Christian than a lazy Lutheran because we have theology behind it. Saved how? By _____ through _____ not _____. Lutherans never hesitate to fill in those blanks with verve. So, what must you do? Nothing! Perhaps one reason some Lutheran-Christians develop this deficiency is because we stop reading too soon. There's a reason the Holy Spirit moved Paul to add the words we call verse 10: "For we are God's handiwork, created in Christ Jesus to do good works, which God prepared in advance for us to do" (NIV). If you peel back the English word *handiwork* and dig into the Greek beneath, we find a word that sounds like our English word *poem*. God is the poet; we are the living poems of God, the works of art, the masterpieces of God. From the perspective of eternity, God sees us habituating the perfect righteousness we receive from Jesus. From the perspective of the here and now, we are, of course, works in progress.

HOLY SPIRIT, SPEAK TO OUR SPIRITS AND STRENGTHEN US. WE DESIRE TO HEAR YOU AND TO BELIEVE THE PROMISES THAT COME FROM JESUS OUR REDEEMER. WE WANT TO GROW IN OUR FAITH. DESPITE ALL THE CHALLENGES THAT WE FACE, WE NEED TO NOT LET OUR HEARTS BE TROUBLED NOR SHOULD WE BE AFRAID. WE ARE CHILDREN OF A LOVING GOD WHO LEADS US BY THE SPIRIT THROUGH THE DIFFICULT SEASONS OF THIS LIFE INTO LIFE FOREVER WITH JESUS. AMEN.

Receiving More

As the subtitle of this book suggests, prepositions possess power: "in, with, and under" were some of Martin Luther's favorite words when he was talking sacramentally—that is, talking about what happens when God's Word meets water or bread and wine. The very presence of Jesus is offered with redemptive forgiveness for the community of the Christ-confessors. We are passive participants in this miracle, a position that is difficult for Westerners, with our culture of achievement and self-sufficiency. Spiritually speaking, however, there are no self-made men or women. It's all about what God has done for us. But what God has done for us is not for *only* us! We are meant for more. We seek arenas to gear up with the full armor of God (Ephesians 6:13–17) and put our faith in action.

In the old city of Turku, on the southwest coast of Finland, stands a bulwark of a built-on-the-rock type of Lutheran cathedral, dating back to the thirteenth century. This rugged building could easily be the photographic dictionary depiction of "A Mighty Fortress." In one of the side altars of this mighty edifice hangs a vulnerable yet venerable crucifix, shockingly without any arms, which means obviously no hands either. Where are the hands of the body of Christ? The answer is us! Through the craft of our hands, God's work is done on earth. The Church is the Body of Christ, but Christ is the life of the Body. The Church gives to the world, but the hands with which we give are themselves gifted by God. Into our hands, the Giver places tools—instruments for designing ideas, cultivating raw materials, and completing our projects. Work was not originally meant to be cursed by "thorns and thistles" (Genesis 3:18). The dilemmas that snake their way into the workplace, complicate even mundane tasks, and take their toll on workers are not the Creator's intent. Even worse, in the midst of these challenges, some are further deprived of the tools they need, sufficient materials to accomplish the task, or even ordinary access to opportunity.

We are all created in the image of God, according to Genesis 1:26–27. Every one of us, from every place on this planet, is a "created co-creator," to use Philip Hefner's term. We're made to be relational and functional. We're made to be makers, crafters—created in Christ Jesus, according to Ephesians 2:10, to do good works as God's masterpieces, God's *poema* in the Greek; poems of the divine poet, prized masterworks of the eternal crafter whose hands work in every generation like the ancients did with primal simplicity.

It all reverberates with biblical, primal simplicity, like the metaphoric material Jesus uses to talk about God's reign. Listen to these ordinary things: seeds and sheep and wind and rain and coins and kings and children and farmers and fields and wheat and weeds and sowers and bread and fish and wine and virgins and water. Ordinary things given. An extraordinary holiness received.

18

LEADING MORE

The anatomy of effective leadership is defined first by a faithful heart and a wise ear, then by a discerning eye with a vision of a flourishing future often requiring gutsy decisions. I can't see this having much to do with the quick results, slick strategies, or the trending tricks of the latest gurus. The struggle is real. The course is long. Tears will flow. Blood will be shed.

Choices matter. Leaders are heedful of life's "contingent moments"—those decisional crossroads of a narrative that are determinative, that set the course of life, and that typically cannot be duplicated or reversed. Leadership is about making choices in, with, and under the ordinariness of challenge and changes.

Choices and Challenges

The worst possible choice is often to make no choice. However, sometimes in life, you don't get the option for a good choice; you have a bad choice or a worse choice. All choices have consequences. Each choice we make narrows the world of possibility for future choices. We are constrained by earlier choice—for good or for ill—either made by the individuals themselves or made by others that affect us.

Take the man by the Pool of Bethesda (John 5). He seemed to take the path of no choice, waiting by the poolside to be healed—thirty-eight long years of waiting and inaction. But Jesus brought healing and prodded the man to action: "Get up, take up your bed, and walk. . . . See, you are well! Sin no more, that nothing worse may happen to you" (John 5:8, 14).

No surprise that your best effort to do what's right will encounter both chronic obstructionists ("negaholics," addicted to negativity) and a spattering of minor-league haters. I've been in leadership long enough not only to expect them but actually to plan for them. Focus first on those who are easy to overlook: those standing with you, speaking well of you, critiquing you constructively and directly, even while desiring to cheer publicly your efforts. The trickier ones, the heartbreaking ones for whom you need spiritual discernment, are those who masquerade to your face as if everything's cool but are spineless backstabbers. The best strategy to deal with them is longevity. Patiently stay the course; their true colors and yours, as the song says, will shine through—yours as you rise, theirs to their demise.

Working among real humans is messy, requiring leaders with a heart—by which I mean a blend of rock-solid integrity and razor-sharp intuition. They know their context and love their people. They have developed an aptitude for the optimum timing in decision making. They have a habit of life that evokes trust in others. They are women and men with a levelheaded sense of fairness, a personal commitment to self-discipline, and a deep reservoir of faith enabling them to move forward without regard to the popularity of their positions. Aristotle recognized this when he spoke of the prime virtues of justice, temperance, and courage. The more uncompromising leaders are with respect to these attributes, the less likely they are to be compromised by favoritism and phoniness; by scandals of power, money, or sex; or by the inevitable pettiness that plagues the human condition.

Three decades ago, I was discussing with a colleague one low-performing student at Concordia College—New York who nonetheless went on to accomplish much good in his life. The distinguished late dean Thomas Green carefully remarked: "He was reluctant to dedicate himself to certain academic tasks."

"Meaning what?" I inquired in response.

"Meaning, he was quite adept . . . well, at being a source of enjoyment in the community and quite deficient in committing to anything but that," the good dean clarified with respectful precision.

We have a responsibility to respect all people, even those who disrespect themselves by disrespecting us or others. The dean worked hard to accomplish that. We also have commensurate responsibility not to permit disrespecters to treat us, others, or themselves—all created in God's image—disrespectfully. Now that's a delicate, if not impossible, dance!

Expecting others to respect you when you don't respect yourself isn't much different than false advertisers expecting others to purchase their product when they themselves have never purchased it. Every human is worth the investment of respecting himself or herself. The key to self-control (with anything) is self-respect, meaning respecting your own body, mind, and soul. Showing respect to yourself today helps to keep your future healthy.

Making More of Every Opportunity

Most people possess some perspective about how to improve humanity. Possessing a point of view on this topic is neither uncommon nor itself problematic. However, we must take care to manage that point of view in a manner that contributes to the quality of human life together. What's rare and needed in our times are people who not only have a point of view but who also are committed to processing their point of view to make a difference in the world. Such processing requires care, wisdom, and precision. As Paul puts it, "Be very careful, then, how you live—not as unwise but as wise, making the most of every opportunity, because the days are evil" (Ephesians 5:15–16 NIV).

Difference-makers know what day it is. They have a sense of time, a perception of timing, a critical awareness of the right moment. Difference-makers do not merely brandish their belief in a private circle and shout down outsiders with their truth. They carry their conviction to the marketplace of ideas; they test it publicly. They do not run from difficult exchanges with difficult audiences. They speak concretely about the practical implications and applications of their ideas.

If you are a Christian thought-leader, a difference-maker who cares about the cause of Christ, you will clothe your ideas with love, because concern for other persons as created in the image of God will move us to ask the Holy Spirit's help to use us to captivate their hearts, fire their imaginations, and mobilize them for active lives of discipleship; therefore, it takes more than just repeating your point—no matter how true—with increasing force, like a sledgehammer. Doing that is to become "a noisy gong" (1 Corinthians 13:1), an ear-numbing, headache-making clatter that's a pleasure to leave behind. It's not easy to make a difference if people are in retreat from you, your words, and your invitation to follow. Leaders need to know both what motivates people and how to make things happen.

In 2005, I copresented a lecture in the MBA program at Cornerstone University in Grand Rapids, Michigan, with Jerry Zandstra, a friend, entrepreneur, and pastor in the Christian Reformed Church. Our emphasis was on what nonprofits and for-profits can learn from each other. For-profits need to learn that people are motivated by more than money. The *more* is mission, vision, and making an impact for humanity, all of which gives people a sense of purpose and a chance to connect their passion with service. Nonprofits, on the other hand, need to learn that good business practices—such as metrics, flowcharts, cash-flow projections, strategic plans, training seminars, and assessment tools—help to carry out the mission. Both nonprofits and for-profits must engage the best practices of business, meaning the highest of standards, detailed accountability, transparency, and verifiability. We must neither be ostrichlike, burying our heads in the sand by paying no attention to markets, nor swinelike, burying all our assets in the vehicles of profit without respect to the way our money is made or people are treated.

Those of us who find ourselves, sometimes surprisingly, in positions of authority also need the occasional attitude check—perhaps especially with regard to the so-called troublemakers among us. Difference-makers understand the value of some people who are pegged to be "troublemakers." Rather than strategically undermining them or wishing they'd poof-be-gone, we should work to listen to these inconvenient challengers. While our egos might feel like those people are bruising our self-image of heroism, the debate they introduce might be just the spark the organization needs. Heirs of Martin Luther's legacy ought to know this better than most. Contemporary rebels are often no more nefarious than many of our foreparents in faith. Consider the revolutionary founders of the United States. Every era tends to exaggerate the propriety of their own way of doing things, the uniformity of a golden past, and the immorality of those who are currently bucking their system.

How is wishing inconvenient challengers would poof-be-gone not a form of murder? We may be shocked that many of those we kill in this way are with us at the resurrection—which is why repentance is a central word in our lexicon.

Following More

Faith-based organizations are often characterized by overattentiveness to leadership—books, conferences, mentoring cohorts. The curious irony for people of faith is that their sacred traditions say more about follow-ship and discipleship, and yet they have an overabundance of materials and resources directed at leadership. But leaders must also learn to be followers—that is, we must pay attention to the wisdom of those who came before us.

We are lost when we stop learning from the past. For most of history, humans lived as though our lives were about more than just our needs, our hopes, our own goals. For generations, we lived with a grandeur that comes only from gratitude, a thankfulness for ancestors who suffered and sacrificed to get us to where we are, to this future of unimaginable blessings that too many take for granted. That's because, for most of human history, our ancestors were attentive to their foreparents, honoring their legacies in ways that led them to make decisions on behalf of their children and the future, on behalf of us, their progeny, their tribe, the unborn heirs who would reap the benefits or bear the consequences of their legacy.

This presents us with an opportunity to reflect: Am I being a good steward of the gifts from those who came before me? Am I considering the consequences of my choices for those who will come after me? Through ease of transportation and access to technology, we are more connected to our contemporary world than any past generation could have dreamed being connected to its, and effective leaders use that connection to promote unity and mutuality in their words and actions. They coordinate common responses, inspired by common sense, pointing toward a sense of our common human destiny. But to fully realize our more, we must also think more about our longitudinal connectivity—connecting to those who came before and those who will come after—as well as our spiritual connectivity to the God of history, who entered time in Jesus to redeem those of us who are lost in time and no longer learning from the Holy Spirit.

We must walk in new ways, along new paths, or we will never see the answer to how we can live together better while following Jesus. Wound up and bound up in every challenge are opportunities we often miss because our eyes are not fixed on Jesus and instead are fixated inside of comfortable old ruts—the ruts of seeing ourselves as victims or as untalented or as too old or too young, for example. The ancients were wise to say, "You go the direction you look." Every day, no matter how dismal, is packed with the fresh promises of Easter. Consider this: In which new direction is God's Spirit calling me to follow Him as I redirect my energy?

More Wisdom

Leaders who have learned leadership through faithful follow-ship will generate wisdom.

Despite the availability of more information than we can meaningfully process, despite the illusion of being knowledgeable—often driven by technology and science—wisdom takes longer to acquire than any one lifetime, which is why we need traditions, rituals, mentors, communities, and institutions. Our highly mobile society doesn't permit the rootage we need.

I mentioned earlier my helpful mirror with the words "It's not about you." This reminder is for leaders as well. Leaders give away the credit and take the blame without permitting themselves to become absorbed by the inevitable loneliness of leadership.

In a simple animal shed, the Son of God was born to a humble virgin. I'm sure Mary often felt alone—unmarried and on the road while pregnant with a child who required lots of explaining. God's chosen ones can feel like voices crying in the wilderness, unheard, out of step, uncool, alone.

If that's the way you sometimes feel, you are in good company. Moses was alone when leading the exodus; Ruth was alone in Moab before meeting Naomi; Elijah was alone during the wicked reign of King Ahab; the widow of Zarephath was alone when "the brook dried up, because there was no rain in the land" (1 Kings 17:7); Mary must have felt alone as a pregnant teenager magnifying the Lord (Luke 1:46–55) in an outlying corner of a mighty empire. And many of us feel alone as we face this world of personal financial crises, of diseases with no known cure, of dreams that have crumbled to dust in the palm of our hands, of ailing and failing parents, of leaders who disappoint us bitterly, of complicated relationships, of families that seem to be fracturing, of desperate prayers that seem to go nowhere. We could add that Jesus must have felt alone in the godforsaken place of His execution. But this Jesus is the location of lavish love, bloodied and beaten, but the fullness of God dwelling bodily (Colossians 2:9).

Jesus is the exemplar of leadership who calls His followers to live by dying, win by losing, and gain by giving.

GRACIOUS GOD, WE PRAISE YOU FOR BEING A GOD WHOSE FEET HAVE FELT THE DUST OF DEATH, WHOSE FLESH WAS FISSURED BY RUSTY SPIKES, AND YET WHOSE HEART HAS NEVER EMPTIED OF COMPASSION. BECAUSE YOU KNOW OUR HUMAN CONDITION, O MERCIFUL SAVIOR, WE ASK YOU TO VISIT US WITH SOOTHING FOR FEVERED BROWS, WITH QUIETUDE FOR TERRIFIED IMAGINATIONS, AND WITH CLARITY OF MIND FOR ALL LEADERS. GUARD THOSE, GOOD SHEPHERD, WHO BRING HEALING ON THE FRONT LINES OF CONTAGION. PROTECT ALL FIRST RESPONDERS AND SAVE THE SOULS OF THOSE TODAY VISITED BY DEATH. O FORGIVING GOD, FOCUS US DAILY ON THE THREE SPLASHES OF PROMISE, WHICH DROWN ALL FAILURE AND FEAR IN THE DEATH AND RESURRECTION OF JESUS CHRIST. AND FINALLY, WITH OUR WORLD BEING SO ASPHYXIATED BY THE ANXIETIES OF THESE DAYS, BREATHE INTO US YOUR SPIRIT, SO THAT WE MIGHT BECOME PUBLIC SIGNS OF YOUR LIFE–GIVING LOVE. IN THE NAME OF JESUS CHRIST. AMEN.

19

TURNED AROUND FOR MORE

O n February 22, 1963, something happened to me that I don't consciously remember but I won't ever spiritually forget. My parents loved me and wanted me to meet their God, so they carried me to St. John Methodist Church in Montego Bay, Jamaica, where I was baptized. It was *the* turnaround moment of my life.

By "turnaround" I mean not only the kind of change that happens in the lives of those who are baptized; I also mean the Ancient Church word *repent*. Repent—rhyming with Advent and Lent, two seasons in which the church emphasizes the renewal that comes with a spiritual turnaround. *Repent*—rhyming with being penitent, another word that does more than rhyme but suggests God's invitation to believers to turn back to Him. "Return to the LORD your God, for He is gracious and merciful, slow to anger, and abounding in steadfast love; and He relents over disaster" (Joel 2:13).

People ask me how to pronounce my name. Since it's been anglicized from Portuguese, Nunes is pronounced like the "newness" of life we have in Christ. Romans 6:4 puts it like this: "We were buried therefore with [Christ Jesus] by baptism into death, in order that, just as Christ was raised from the dead by the glory of the Father, we too might walk in *newness* of life" (my emphasis).

How often do you get that new life, that opportunity at a new start? According to the Lutheran tradition, we get it every day! In three splashes in the threefold name, Father, Son, and Spirit, that love is made as real as the water.

In his Ninety-Five Theses, Luther emphasized that the entire Christian life is marked by baptismal turning and returning to the Lord. The first of Luther's theses states: "When our Lord and Master Jesus Christ said, 'Repent' [Matt. 4:17], he willed the entire life of believers to be one of repentance."[57] And as Luther further explained in the Large Catechism, Baptism gives us "grace, the Spirit, and power to suppress" the sinful nature in us, so that our new nature in Christ "may come forth and become strong."[58]

The Anatomy of a Turnaround

Those who have been turned around by Jesus Christ often specialize in leading organizational turnarounds as well. There's something poignant in seeing oneself as an agent for the care and redemption of all that God has made. There's something unassailable about believing that nothing and no one is too far down to be brought up, too far out to be brought in, too far removed to be redeemed.

One analogy from the sports world highlights this. On January 3, 2019, the St. Louis Blues had the worst record in the National Hockey League. They were in dead-last place among the thirty-one teams in the NHL. They lost more games than they won. On June 12, 2019, they won the Stanley Cup as the best team in the National Hockey League. How did they execute their turnaround? You will recognize many of these themes from parts of this book:

1. Imagination. They reimagined a preferred future that included winning more games and losing fewer games. They pursued this future intentionally, one game at a time.

2. Collaboration. They collaborated in new ways of working together—new strategies, new plays, new players.

---

57   *LW* 31:25.

58   LC IV 76.

3. Investing in People. They didn't invest in their future or trade away key players for future years' draft considerations; instead, they invested in the remainder of their 2019 season. And they began by working with who they had on their team.

4. Accountability. They raised levels of responsibility—especially with respect to their defensive game, even bringing in a rookie goaltender—and they started winning more games than they lost.

5. Celebration! Several players were at a bar in the midst of their losing, and they heard the 1980s pop hit "Gloria" by Laura Branigan. They vowed they'd blast it after every winning game. Sometimes, even in the midst of a tough season, you've got to celebrate the small victories—and they will begin to accumulate.

Diligence Flows from Repentance

Deep down, we sense that God is up to something good in each of us. We are meant for more than four score years followed by death. Splashed in the name of the Father, Son, and Spirit, we become God's children; echoing across the waters of Baptism is a primal invitation with each of our names on it. We are called, claimed, and dispatched into life with deep purpose at every age and stage. A calling is something we should remember daily as we make the sign of the cross and then launch into life, putting that calling into practice. "Be all the more diligent to confirm your calling and election, for if you practice these qualities you will never fall" (2 Peter 1:10).

It can be discouraging when our sense of calling doesn't become clearly evident or apparent to us. A student emailed me about the unfairness and unhappiness in life, which had left her shuddering in restlessness, wondering gloomily whether there was any hope, any plan, any rhyme or reason to life. Here was my email answer to her:

I'm sorry that I have no blueprint. It just seems that the human quest for fairness, not to mention the pursuit of happiness, results far too often in the exact opposite—experiences of injustice and sadness. What I am convinced about, however, is that the fact of our frustration itself should prompt us never to quit striving, but to press even deeper into the truth that we are meant for more than we could ever ask or imagine (Ephesians 3:20) and that this world's experiments of doing life apart from the divine design have overpromised and underdelivered. Jesus' words about seeking first God's realm and God's righteousness (Matthew 6:33) imply that we should be careful about what we are chasing after in life. And when we hunger and thirst for the right things, the things that Jesus prioritizes, that's a sign that the Spirit is already at work in us, bringing into view the fullness that Jesus promises: All these things that you most deeply need will be given to you (see Matthew 6:33). That's the best answer I have. Remain diligent!

Know that when something is profoundly wrong in your life, when there's an inexplicable hitch, an obstacle on your path, there is a reason—always! Ask God, what is this about? What am I to learn? What do I need to see? How will this test today lead to a testimony tomorrow? What's the change in me or around me You want to see? What's the change I must initiate? How are You using this cross I bear, Lord, to shape me, conform me?

I have shared with fellow presidents in the Concordia University System, as well as with various mentors, colleagues, and friends, that the calendar year of 2019 represented by far the toughest period in this job, which, overall, is the toughest position I have held in my life. The complexity of untangling successfully and reversing irreversibly the interconnected pressures facing Concordia College—New York is at some level daunting but not at all dispiriting. On the contrary, the Holy Spirit has used these tough times to teach me some existential lessons.

During one particularly problematic month, LCMS President Matthew Harrison directed me to the Formula of Concord, Article XI, paragraphs 48–49. I entirely recommend this. The same God who set eternity in human hearts has also "before the foundation of the world" (Ephesians 1:4) predetermined what problems and pain would work on us to shape us into the image of God's Son. I love the pattern in the Hebrew of Ecclesiastes 3:11:

ha'olam—foreverness, eternity

natan—God has set, placed, gifted

belibbam—in human hearts

Baptism is the visible assurance of that invisible gift. Baptism sets us into our various vocations. Not a vacation—which suggests disengagement from workaday activity—nor an occupation—which implies a job or employment—but vocation, which means "calling," from the Latin verb *vocare*. Resting on the assurance of our Baptism, we can live diligently in our callings to the end.

A Sinking Ship

Stephen Fox wrote a book called *Transatlantic*, in which he chronicles the voyages of famous steamships across the Atlantic Ocean. He discusses those ocean liners that claimed unsinkability yet sank, such as the *Titanic* and the *Lusitania*. I was struck by his description of that moment when everybody left aboard a sinking ship knows they're doomed. All the lifeboats have left; the vessel is taking on water; catastrophe is inevitable. There may be an hour or two left, but everybody knows they're going to die. Some sing hymns, some scream for help, some pray silently, some play immoral games, some just hold hands, but there is a moment when mortality is in your face. It doesn't pay to put your trust in dust or in things that rust when death is in your face.

Perhaps it's for the sake of psychological survival in the midst of tough times, but we live in a world of euphemistic doublespeak, especially when we talk about death. We expect the descriptive words, metaphors, and adjectives to soften the gut punch of bad things happening to us. Think of the ways in which we try to soften the sledgehammer of death and grief, calling it "passing on," "passing away," "going to a better place" (which sometimes is true), or "earning your wings" (which never is true). The longer I live, the more I prefer the plainspoken way of calling things what they are. The more candid the characterization, in my mind, the better chance at developing an accurate plan for responding to the problem, the pain, the crisis, the negative event, and extracting from it the lesson God has in mind for us. Thesis 21 of Luther's Heidelberg Disputation speaks directly against religious sugarcoating: "A theologian of glory calls evil good and good evil. A theologian of the cross calls the thing what it actually is."[59]

So, let's speak plainly. Yes, life can collapse without warning. Natural disasters seem to be on the rise, or at least are more publicized. Most people living in extreme poverty suffer from the multigenerational catastrophe of an underdevelopment of resources. These long-term living hells won't be remedied by philosophical analysis or redeemed by externally implemented quick fixes. While I worked for Lutheran World Relief, walking alongside vulnerable communities, I arrived at the hypothesis that the "solution" to suffering is often hidden inside the problem, especially as local treasures, local talent, and local resources are recognized, liberated, and deployed. There is something sacramental in this approach. God works through the living Word weaving its way in, with, and under life's starkest realities to bring about meaningful change.

The Extraordinariness of Water

Through ordinary water, God brings about the most meaningful change for Christians—one that sets us free and shapes how we live and how we die. As I once heard Bishop Mark Hanson preach: "In Baptism we have already died the ultimate death, leaving us free to risk every other death for the sake of the life of the world."

My friend Reed Lessing, a pastor-theologian and preacher extraordinaire living in Minnesota, pointed out to me the thematic prevalence of ordinary water in John's Gospel. So, I went drilling, and here's what I discovered:

---

59 *LW* 31:40.

- In John 1, John the Baptist, baptizing with ordinary water down by the Jordan River, sees Jesus and makes the extraordinary confession: "Behold! Check this out, for real! The Lamb of God, who takes away the sin of the world!"

- In John 2, Jesus expedites the fermentation process at a wedding where the wine ran dry, making the most extraordinary wine from ordinary water.

- In John 3, an inquisitive leader named Nicodemus comes to Jesus under the cover of dark, at night—Nick at Night—understandably concerned, as neither he nor his mother were very much interested in his entering the womb a second time. Then, Jesus explains being born again, answering, "Very truly, I tell you, no one can enter the kingdom of God without being born of water and Spirit."

- In John 4, Jesus meets a much-marred, much-maligned, much-married woman at a well and tells her, "If you drink of the water that I will give you, you will never be thirsty again!"

- In John 5, a man has been overlooked and left behind for thirty-eight long years at the side of the pool and has never gotten into the allegedly healing water; then Jesus, the fount of life, tells him to stand again: "Take up your mat and walk."

- In John 6, Jesus walks on water—without the aid of water skis—and tells you and me and the disciples, "It is I; do not be afraid." Whatever it is that you're going through, do not be afraid.

- In John 7, "on the last day of the feast," the greatest day, the high point after seven days of merrymaking, eating, and drinking, Jesus has the audacity to say to them: "If anyone is thirsty—if there's a gap, if there's a void, something missing in your life—come to Me and drink, and out of your heart shall flow rivers of living water, flowing for those who still need a holy touch."

- Then in John 19, Jesus is on the cross, and water flows from His pierced side.

JOHN THE BAPTIST

From the first chapter of the Bible, when the Spirit is hovering over the waters, to the last chapter, when John says, "And let the one who is thirsty come; let the one who desires take the water of life without price" (Revelation 22:17), water is life-giving, life-enhancing, life-restoring in the biblical narrative. As we live out our vocations, work to right wrongs in Jesus' name, and even as we die, the Holy Spirit is extraordinarily at work in, with, and under the ordinary water, enabling us to cling to God's promises forever.

20

SEEKING MORE

The restlessness that lurks in all persons, while sometimes misdirected, originates in God. It drives us to delve deeply, to attempt to decode the purpose of our lives, our "meant for more-ness." But prior to that, seekers like us were first sought. Before we could seek, the Spirit in His goodness and mercy first sought us and then caught us, like little fishes, in, with, and under the water of baptismal grace, where the blood-bought promises of Christ were sent in, with, and under the Word to flow through every day of our lives.

This narrative repeats throughout the history of salvation. God pursues us all, and we are like Adam and Eve in their garden of querulous disobedience. At one level or another, we all hide from God. Then God asks us a three-word (in English) question: "Where are you?" (Genesis 3:9). The original Hebrew has just one word: *ayekah*? "People, where is your head?" "Where do you think you are?" "Where do you think you're going?" "What is it, precisely, that you think you're doing with your life, or rather with the life I've given to you?"

Have you ever felt like you've gotten ahead of God, gotten outside of God's space of grace? Are you, perhaps even today, walking ahead of God? Be comforted to know that you are not out of God's sight. God sees you, and He never relents in seeking you. The familiar English line of Psalm 23 says that "goodness and mercy shall follow me all the days of my life" (v. 6), but goodness and mercy do so much more than merely *follow* us! The Hebrew verb here suggests that God's goodness and mercy *pursue* us. From that infinite initiative where we are first pursued and sought, we can become lifelong seekers.

Quite naturally, we yield to selfish preoccupation rather than the more for which we are meant. Quite instinctively, we focus on the more we meant to get rather than the more we're sent to give. Though our old selves are drowned in the turnaround waters of Baptism, they are really good swimmers. So, with quite the self-sabotage, we miss our calling—because vocation usually comes from the outside in, not the inside out. It comes from God, who calls out to us: "Where are you?"

In the Old Testament, Joseph was once seeking as well. Then "a man found him wandering in the fields. And the man asked him, 'What are you seeking?'" (Genesis 37:15). I wonder how we might answer that question. Some of us have been wandering for years, maybe decades, unwilling to be found. Some of us have been searching for something we can't find words to describe, bouncing from job to job, from bed to bed, from church to church, from website to website. Exactly what is it you are seeking today?

Faith is opening your eyes and seeing a trail of evidence tracking through your life and pointing toward that which cannot be seen. Martin Luther put it this way: "We must have inner eyes of faith."[60] These eyes both see and seek the promises of God with a faith that clings for life. Like the promise that God loves you in Jesus Christ and Christ forgives you without your deserving it. The promise that the Holy Spirit will not leave you alone, but that this breath of God is as close as the very . . . next . . . breath . . . you . . . will . . . take. Sometimes, it seems as if we have ridiculed childlike faith so much that we have lost our ability to believe in anything or anyone or any hope or any dream anymore. Returning to our childlike faith in the simple truth of the Gospel, we are reminded that we are both *meant* for more and, even more, we are *sent* to call others to discover their more as they recognize God's disposition toward all people: "The LORD is merciful and gracious, slow to anger and abounding in steadfast love" (Psalm 103:8). The Gospel is always an evangelistic gift. See God's gift to you and then seek to be a gift. See differently. Seek to live differently. See your neighbor. Seek to be a neighbor.

---

60 *LW* 3:196.

Touching More

O GOD OF GRACE AND GLORY, YOUR TOUCH OF MERCY CHANGES EVERYTHING. YOUR SAVING TOUCH OPENS THE EVERLASTING DOOR, LEADING US FROM DEATH TO LIFE. BECAUSE OF THIS HOPE YOU HAVE GIVEN US, WE PRAISE YOUR NAME AND WE WORK TO LOVE EVERYONE, ESPECIALLY OUR NEIGHBORS WHO NEED YOUR TOUCH. IN JESUS. AMEN.

I was touched to the point of tears by the applause directed toward the casket of one of my mentors and heroes of faith, Richard John Neuhaus. While alive, he spoke and wrote with facile precision, forceful eloquence, cutting raillery. The reader could almost hear the satirical tongue in cheek when Neuhaus sensed a contradiction of argument. Despite his popularity, he was generous in taking my phone calls, giving me advice, and offering me an endorsement for my 1999 book *Voices from the City*. At his funeral Mass, those who were assembled gave a standing ovation unto God for the gift of a life well lived. The Lord Jesus Himself was no stranger to human suffering. Those who were grieving experienced His presence. They heard His words of consolation and comfort. They felt His touch. They rejoiced in His healing.

> Soon afterward He went to a town called Nain, and His disciples and a great crowd went with Him. As He drew near to the gate of the town, behold, a man who had died was being carried out, the only son of his mother, and she was a widow, and a considerable crowd from the town was with her. And when the Lord saw her, He had compassion on her and said to her, "Do not weep." Then He came up and touched the bier, and

the bearers stood still. And He said, "Young man, I say to you, arise." And the dead man sat up and began to speak, and Jesus gave him to his mother. Fear seized them all, and they glorified God, saying, "A great prophet has arisen among us!" and "God has visited His people!" And this report about Him spread through the whole of Judea and all the surrounding country. (Luke 7:11–17)

Jesus touched the casket. That touch changed everything. For the religious ritualists looking on, that touch made Jesus impure. For the dead son occupying the casket, that touch restored him to life. For the mother decimated by grief, that touch restored her hope for the future. For those carrying the coffin, that touch shut them up in stunned awe. For those in the surrounding areas who heard the narrative, that touch sent waves of praise to God "through the whole of Judea and all the surrounding country."

Jesus' touch is powerful, and He touches our lives too—for example, when Jesus' words "Do not weep" and "Arise!" enter our ears and hearts. Or in the Holy Meal, when Jesus' presence in, with, and under bread and wine enters our mouths and strengthens our faith. When Jesus' encouragement surrounds us in, with, and under the Body of Christ, the fellowship, the church, our Christian friends. Now consider ways we, like the people of Luke 7 who witnessed Jesus' touch, can also spread that news "through the whole of [insert your village or neighborhood here] and all the surrounding country"!

Seeing More

"I will see the goodness of the LORD in the land of the living!" (Psalm 27:13). In 1986, I evinced one of my first attempts to talk publicly about Jesus. After my effort, which was more earnest than effective, a graduate of Concordia College—New York, Pastor George Loewer, offered his discernment: "John, try not to be so heavenly minded that you ain't no earthly good." By this, he meant to preach with your eyes wide open, not mired in myopic intellectualism, not stuffed with otherworldly terminology. See the everyday ways God works. Never lose sight of the radical vision—John the Evangelist described it as "the Word became flesh" (John 1:14); the hymnwriter Christopher Wordsworth described it as "God in flesh made manifest." For the first time in world history, human eyes beheld God. They saw, literally, "the goodness of the Lord"—who is Jesus—"in the land of the living."

Where is this place? According to *The Lutheran Study Bible*, the "land of the living" refers not to heaven but to this world, this life. Precisely where we live, love, work, play, and pray is the land where you can expect to see God. The mission of Jesus, both heavenly minded and desiring earthly good, never swerves from either God's holy plan nor veers from the ordinary people to whom God's love is directed. It's perfectly both. What greater sight for sore eyes than the glory of God in Jesus—both fully human and fully divine!

Dr. Alvin L. Barry, born in 1931, died rather suddenly on March 23, 2001. When he was president of The Lutheran Church—Missouri Synod, he and I had a business conversation for Concordia Publishing House about a month before his death about a book he wanted to write on the topic of heaven called *Oh, What a Surprise*. He was insistent about the title.

"Why?" I asked him. Ordinarily, the title flows from the writing, from what's written, not the other way around.

He then told me: "Well, when my wife, Jean, was dying [in 1996], she was taking what we thought was her last breath, and she closed her eyes. Then suddenly she again opened her eyes and with a look of indescribable joy fixed on her face, she said these final words: 'Oh, what a surprise.'" Much like the song sung by Al Jolson in the 1927 movie *The Jazz Singer*, we ain't seen nuthin' yet. Oh, what a surprise.

One thing leads to another: conception leads to birth, birth leads to sin, sin leads to death, Christ gives us faith, and believing in a God we can't see will lead one day to seeing the God who is beyond belief. In the interim, we carry our cross. No surprise there.

Only by carrying the cross can we build bridges, linking arms with people who feel they are outside of God's love and God's justice. We begin in our own ordinary communities—right here where we live, love, work, pray, and play, right here where we post and comment on social media networks. Animated by the Spirit, we speak truth in love; we march on with backs straight yet with humility; we do justice with mercy, undistracted by the zealotry of the crowds. Our faces are set like flint, standing together and believing together that a day will come when people will not be judged by their titles or their tribes or their shortcomings! The day will come when people are not racialized nor minoritized. So, we cling to the name that is above every name, the name that motivates us toward the more for which we are meant; Him we proclaim: Jesus Christ, our Lord! As we stay our way through life's afflictions, we discover a quantum fact of faith: Where human "strength ends," Luther said in his exposition on the Magnificat, "God's strength begins."[61] Faith doesn't come from our persistent walking or work; we are graced into it (see Ephesians 2:8–10). We are fed on the journey. As Herb Brokering penned it: "Bless our bread, open our eyes: Jesus, be our great surprise."[62]

Paul, at his most virtuosic, penned this based on Isaiah 64:4: "'What no eye has seen, what no ear has heard, and what no human mind has conceived'—the things God has prepared for those who love Him" (1 Corinthians 2:9 NIV). Let's dwell on that together:

Song has not been sung, poem has not been composed, engineer has never designed, navigator has never discovered, code writer has never digitized, chemist has never concocted, builder has never constructed, preacher has never captured in words what God has prepared—a place with no more loneliness, no more dying, no more getting lied to or lied about, no more losing, no more bruising, no more fearing, no more fighting over foolishness, no more waiting and watching and weeping, only seeing and being beheld and held in the gaze of God forever in the name of Father, Son, and Spirit. Amen.

---

61 *LW* 21:340.

62 Herb Brokering, "Stay with Us," stanza 1.